Tonal-Vibrations

*A one-man's spiritual journey
towards self-discovery*

John Meyer

authorHOUSE®

AuthorHouse™
1663 Liberty Drive, Suite 200
Bloomington, IN 47403
www.authorhouse.com
Phone: 1-800-839-8640

First published by AuthorHouse 9/15/2008

ISBN: 978-1-4343-8438-6 (sc)
ISBN: 978-1-4343-8439-3 (hc)

Library of Congress Control Number: 2008908100

Printed in the United States of America
Bloomington, Indiana

This book is printed on acid-free paper.

Dedication

To my mother and father. If it wasn't for their love for each other and the love they have expressed to me, I would not have been able to grow and expand my love within the Divine God, giving me the strength and the ability to journey on this path of self-discovery.

I also want to thank my close friends for putting up with my ranting about my experiences. Thanks to those good friends who took the time to read this manuscript and in giving me the required courage to finish it.

Contents

The Introduction

I have always enjoyed sitting next to a person and listening to their accounts of tales past. I like hearing about what they needed to accomplish and what hurdles they had to overcome to make it to the point where they are now. I enjoy unfolding each experience of their life's events and spreading them out in a linear fashion. Noticing how patterns form from pieces in each event. These ideas pile up upon themselves, forming a deeper, richer story that allows me to view the mind of the storyteller, noticing how individual patterns are collected alongside the perceptions of each event, merging both together and forming their personality. As each new event unfolds, their ever-expanding consciousness changes time and time again, transforming their personalities all over again.

I have often asked myself why I would consider putting my thoughts down on paper. For there are many things floating in my brain at once. At times it feels like I'm sitting there watching a slide show projecting images of moments of my lifetime one by one before my eyes. There are so many things I want to share and express. I find this need cannot be overlooked, this desire to lay out my life and offer it to others as a humble attempt to understand each crevice, to expose my awareness of life and my interactions within it. I can only hope that it gives comfort to some by allowing me to share pieces of my life. My wish is to reach out to someone who has experienced similar things with their life and say to them, "you're not alone in this journey."

I wanted to freeze these special moments of my life upon paper. To lay upon this canvas of pulp my spiritual development and the developing conscious of my mind of who I am and who I am becoming. This will allow me in retrospect to open up those hidden cracks and expose them to the light of my spiritual being, to absorb each experience, build upon it and become a better person. It will allow me to become closer to the answers of who we are and what we will become.

Many of these experiences I've written about happened earlier in my life, and it has taken me close to twenty years to understand the true magnitude of them. With each experience, I took great strides in overcoming limitations imposed upon me by my religious beliefs. I learned not to fear the unfamiliar but to embrace it. I learned to look into that vast expansion of the unknown, learning to understand it for what it is and allowing it to change my belief system accordingly. Eventually I came to the realization that I needed to allow the results of these experiences to refine my tonal vibrations and to allow me to embrace the divinity within.

So I sit here pouring my soul upon these pages, laying my life out in a linear fashion. Exposing my story in the hope that you will find some pieces of my life's puzzle that will fit into the empty spaces in your own. Opening up my innermost thoughts, humbling myself in these words only so you will be able to put more of your puzzle together.

1

Tonal Vibration and Energy Patterns

I wanted to stop right here and express something that needs to be said. I originally wanted to start this manuscript with events in my life, explaining about key segments in my life that brought me to the ideas and beliefs I take as truth. In this sense, this first chapter is out of place. I originally wanted to put this information in the later chapters, but this did not sit right with me. I have felt, even though as dry at times it is, is the one of the key cornerstones in how I developed throughout my life.

I feel this chapter is my Rosetta stone that will continuously be used to interpret each event I write about. Each chapter may appear as totally different events; in time they will eventually and slowly merge together. Applying separate pieces of the puzzle, with each grouping an image forms. Please bear with me on this chapter. What at first it may seem like ideas that are not fully be apparent will flow and merge together with other experiences and allow you as a reader to be enriched. The information here will allow you to understand the rest of this manuscript in greater detail than if it had been moved to a later chapter.

Writing about my past was a tough one. It wasn't because of a tragic event that had happened and that had blocked out sections of my life. This wasn't the case. Later in life I experienced an event that caused my memories to be removed. There are portions of time in the past I can no longer recall. I apologize that this book does not contain at times a more coherent telling of the events of my life. I will do my best to string these things together as best as I can to allow you a more fluid, linear timeframe. If there are any gaps in what I write, I can only attribute them to the missing pieces of my memories, strips of my life that have been forcibly removed from my consciousness.

I feel that what has been excluded from this manuscript does not lessen the stories within it. They would have been an extra ingredient in this creation of a meal to make it that much more of a dining experience; instead I find that it leaves you at times wanting more than what is given. This I too am sorry for.

I have always felt different from everyone else. As far as I can remember I was conscious of things that the five senses could not explain. Things you were taught in school would not even come close to attempt to explain things that happened to me in my daily experiences of life. I knew that people around me would not understand. How would you tell someone close to you that you remember living on this planet as well as others in previous lifetimes? Fragments of lives I have lived have filtered through the thin veil that separates us from our own divinity. Little things would trigger it: seeing a waitress in a restaurant, or noticing a new employee showing up for work for the first time. Totally unrelated fragments would become a part of me for no apparent reason.

I have always had this unique ability to sense energy patterns. I've come to rely on it. I like to compare it to animals sensing planetary shifts and natural disasters. No, I cannot tell when the next stock market crash will be or whom you are going to marry.

What I do sense is the ability to see the energy shifts—vibrations is what I call them. Everyone and everything emits a unique tonal vibration. The compilation of each ones thought collects together to create the rate of there vibrations. In other words, they vibrate at the rate of what they think. This is true throughout everything. Everything vibrates on a molecular and quantum level. As our thoughts change, we too change the rate of tonal vibrations we emit.

Ironically, this frequency is carried over into the afterlife. I have always felt both the living and the deceased. I have experienced vibration levels of angels, archangels, spirit guides, and lost souls. I have observed realms and levels of energy that run parallel to our world. And I have seen energy pattern shifts of our planet earth as we enter into a higher, more refined state of being.

Tonal vibrations are basically broken into two parts. Vibration is the wave pattern that each one of us emits. Tonal is the sound that is emitted as the byproduct of the vibration itself. When you combine both together you get the tonal vibration.

We come into this world with a preset set of contracts that we have chosen to accomplish in order to develop areas of our consciousness, to correct our imperfections and become a greater spiritual being. What better way to grow and learn and become more divine within than to jump into a game board called life, to remove the concept of whom we truly are. Each being separates from their Divinity in order to grow by the direct experiences gained from our events, both good and bad.

This process for one's soul is the accelerated version of growth. By enveloping ourselves with the thick veil of forgetfulness, we cannot see who we truly are. We lose the ability to co-create with all life by thought alone. We need to draw up greater reserves of energy and focus the intent with greater strength to accomplish only a fraction of what we could do when on the other side. By this very process of growth we grow by leaps and bounds. With little changes in our thought patterns, we change our very core of who we are. We continuously refine our energies to sweeten those tones we emit. By the direct experiences of these very processes of trial by fire we are able to change who we are and in turn shift these energy patterns to a more refined, purified state.

I had another ability that I miss today so much. An event in my thirties caused this to be removed from me. In the first half of my life I had the ability to split my consciousness into two separate, independent states of thought. For years I had assumed everyone had this ability and could not understand why people could not think like I did. Imagine being able to concentrate on two things at once with the same intent and focus but also be aware and understand both thoughts simultaneously. It was as though my brain were running two processes in parallel. I could hold a conversation with someone and at the same time concentrate on abstract concepts and ideas, using both halves of my consciousness with equal intent and with the same amount of my conscious thought. I loved the way I could independently but simultaneously jump from one to another, receiving bits of insight and understanding.

I had a talent in my younger years for seeing something and understanding the steps needed to accomplish the task at hand. It was similar to a photographic memory, but instead of recalling pictures of what I had seen in the past, I knew what was needed to accomplish the tasks that were laid out in front of me. I especially loved it when going through school and college. It was wonderful never having to study to retain what was needed for each exam, seeing the problem with its many pieces as well as seeing the required solution, and understanding how each piece fits into the overall scope. Then by merging both my individual minds together and 'zoning out,' I could assemble these ideas and concepts into a working, completed whole. Many times I would look at these things with a single-minded viewpoint and never knew how I was able to accomplish these tasks.

In life and in all the realms and planes of existences beyond what our five senses can perceive, these tonal energies are never constant. By their very nature they change. Through stagnation comes death. The energies need to be constantly changing and continuously moving. Expanding, refining, and compressing, they gain their own unique knowledge and grow in their own right.

Look at your own life. You are not the same person as you were a day, week, or year ago. You need to continuously expand your awareness and express who you are at the moment of time you are in. With this expression we become more aware of our own divinity. As our energy vibrates it expands out from us then mixes with its surroundings and pieces of other people's tonal vibrations are in turn mixed with yours. By this process, in part, interacting with others helps make up who you really are.

Why is it that when you're with someone for a period of time you can finish each other's sentences? Your energies become blended together, and your consciousnesses shift to become more aligned to one thought while at the same time you're still two independent minds.

Each object, place, person, and animal emits its own unique tonal vibration. This continuously blending of energies with the energies surrounding your reality has a greater effect on your own development than you realize. Think on how your mind becomes when listening to a piano or guitar being played. Then let's shift your conscious thought. Now imagine you're surrounded by many vehicles stuck in traffic. Being aware of these blending of energies, one can consciously eliminate and minimize the effect on one's tonal vibration. In doing so you learn lessons on how to mold these energies into something more refined and beneficial to your development.

One of my talents lies in the ability to read the energy signatures of the spoken word. Most people when speaking concentrate on what is being said. What they don't realize is that this is only a portion of what comes out of a person. Visualize a crystal, a multifaceted object. Each side is a flat, linear plane. But on the edges, they are connected. Each of these surfaces are projected at a slight angle from each other. When people hear someone speak, they concentrate on only one of the surfaces and not the entire projection. There are many other sides that are connected to each other.

By expanding beyond the five senses, we begin to see what is truly being spoken. Most of the time it is not the words that are being said but the intent that is attached to these words. The first and most apparent side is of course the spoken word. But the meanings behind them have a smaller impact than what is carried along with it. We know that the words themselves are waves of sound being sent out from the vocal cords into the atmosphere. This can be considered another side of the projection being emitted. In the initial stages of awareness one can feel the waves being sent along with what is being said. It is the same as when you feel a low, thundering base being emitted from a passing vehicle.

The interesting thing is that if you look deeper you will notice something else attached to the edge of these waves of sound; another side or facet will began to emerge. With regard to the intent of the speaker, the very nature of their thought processes not only forms the words and wave links but the energy signature imbedded in each word being spoken. This is what I call the truth behind the words. This energy pattern many times precedes the words by a small amount.

This subtle shift in someone's energy patterns from thoughts sent through the spoken word can have a major impact on someone who has received this projection. Look at someone in your life. Using the same words but applying a subtle change in the energy signature, the impact on the recipient will greatly differ. Praise can quickly become a criticism. The interesting thing is when we mix our thoughts, words, and energy into the wave link and it reaches its intended target, the person's reaction on some level will reverberate back and blend into our tonal vibration. We do not have to see or hear a reaction of what we had said; instead, we feel the response to what we said by the change in the recipient's tonal vibration. A piece of what you gave out mixes with their energy, and the result of that returns and mixes with yours. That is one reason why words cut more deeply that a knife.

There is another flat surface. This is usually on the opposite side of the above-mentioned energy pattern. This facet I would like to think balances out the energy wave. Both work in harmony with each other but yet are still separate from each other. Each human can feel it on some level of their consciousness, but it mainly is hidden from us. This is what I call the tonal vibration. This vibration is the sound that the energy pattern creates. It is a combination of all the other facets I've mentioned to this point. It is an accumulation of all the previous surfaces. The interesting thing with it is that it works in junction with the Divine signature that will be spoken of next. Spirits feel and see this. For it is the core of our being. The accumulation of both the tonal vibration and the divine signature is what each of us resonates, with no two alike.

Let's look at the last of these surfaces, the Divine signature. When going deeper into the spoken word you yet again find another facet hidden from view. This is also attached on the edge of the energy vibrations imbedded within it. This flat surface, though a part of the crystal projection, is largely misunderstood and not commonly used. When used correctly, it can be the strongest side of the spoken word, and some use it without ever knowing they do. It's the energy signature of health. More importantly, it's the reconnection to the divinity within each of us. Using this technique, one is able to re-link someone's divine connection to one's cosmic self. Some would like to refer to it as the communication with God. It allows, if properly done, one to obtain a rest from trials and confusion and to reconnect on a conscious level one's divinity within to the Divine God, the source of all. It gives back one's power to choose to heal physically, mentally, or spiritually, to realign oneself back onto one's chosen path and stabilize the fluctuations in the tonal energy being emitted.

2

The Early Years

It is funny how things work. When I came into this lifetime, a fully formed personality and mindset for this body had not fully formed yet. The tonal vibration needed to accomplish what I set out to do had not been developed. It was missing many experiences, both in the contracts I had chosen and the reaction to everything surrounding my own reality. My higher self had to carefully mold circumstances in my development of my consciousness to change the vibration of my being. I still had to grow into what I needed to do. In other words I had not had experiences in this lifetime to develop my personality and thought patterns.

To compensate, my spiritual being drew from multiple previous lifetimes to form a foundation of who I was. You can see this by looking at the various stages of people around you. When kids are really young, their basic foundation or personality is quite different from what it is in their pre-teens and then teen years. It is through those interactions with the energies around them that they begin to 'grow' into their own being. It often takes till they're in their thirties to fully develop a somewhat stable mindset of who they are and what they will become.

With the abilities given to me by my higher self, I was able to draw upon the experiences and understandings of many lives I had lived and also who I was on the other side. At that time, even though I did not understand what was truly going on, I still understood the bond and love I had with the many guides, angels, and archangels who continually supported me in my development. Feeling them around me at all times coming and going, I knew I was protected from harm.

This especially became apparent when I attended Sunday school. The teacher would explain what was meant by the writings of the Bible and how we needed to interpret it. At the same time I know that they were not correct. I remembered living alongside and following Christ, listening to him teach, and understanding his intentions and how he spoke his truth. I also drew upon the lifetimes of religious lives I'd experienced as a monk, a priest, and even a mystic. When I confronted them about these topics, they became agitated and explained that I was heading straight to hell if I kept these lines of thought up. Firing back, I explained to them that hell was a concept conjured up by the elite few to unite the people toward a common enemy to fight. There is nothing better for a group to bind different walks of people together than by having a common idea or goal. I found out later that this was not the right thing to say to them.

Throughout life and especially in my younger years I battled on many fronts. The first and foremost is that what I perceived was truth by the very experiences of my higher self and my previous lives usually clashed with what I was told by my family, friends, priests, and society. Was I to follow what I knew to be right or was I to follow what society told me to do? It took me twenty-five years to overcome this hurdle and find the truth within. I knew not one person to whom could go to express my distress on what was happening to me at that time. I did not know what tonal vibrations meant or even what energy patterns and signatures were. What I did know is I felt them. I did not know how to put them into words that I could understand. Later in my adult life, as I went into my quest, I envied people I came upon who had the ability to communicate with their spirit guides and angels. I have never felt I found someone who had the same unique ability as I did.

The house I lived in while growing up had many spirits, both good and bad—even earthbound spirits that had not transitioned yet. I was terrified of them. I had sensed their energy signatures, and it became very strong at times. Drawing upon the energies of my higher angels I was able to push back these beings. Even today my sister and I joke about feeling this presence around the house and how we hated to go to the basement. This is where he had stayed for most of the time. This spirit would occasionally come up to the main floor when the higher energy beings were not there. I lived in a converted attic as a bedroom with my two brothers. I asked the archangels to apply a barrier to prevent the earth-bound spirit from entering. After doing this, I found in years to come that the only place of refuge was the bedroom in the attic.

There were many times I would stand at the top of the stairs looking down and see the wall of mist at the doorway and behind it was the earth-bound spirit looking back up. I hated going down to the bathroom at night.

It wasn't uncommon for me to wake up in the middle of the night and see the faces of souls looking back at me. It did not matter if I had my eyes open or closed; they would still be there looking at me. Not understanding what was happening and being afraid of being called a freak if I were to tell someone, I would hide under my covers pretending that this was my shield of protection to ward away any harmful spirits. I had to laugh because the covers never stopped those faces from staring back at me. But somehow I felt it was my only protection. Nothing resulted from it of course, but it would reappear for many years to come.

Many nights I awakened to a spirit standing next to my bed looking at me. They were people I did not know. After repeated occurrences I became used to them and would wave to them, smile, and go back to sleep. Over time I came to understand that these spirits, for whatever reason, would come by to honor me with their visit and go on their way. I knew they would not harm me. Later in life I began to understand that a lot of spirits like to be around people's tonal vibrations. They flock to humans on this earth plane to feel and become a part of the energies people give off. Some find peace, which allows them to transit over to the other side. Others feel comfort and protection in the vibrations you project out. In either case the stronger and more refined you become in your tonal vibration, the more they like to flock around you. Many times I feel the room to be extremely crowded with these spirits.

On one interesting night, I was lying in bed, alone in a room I shared with my brothers, feeling relaxed and just about to drift off to sleep, when I felt that energy shift come. This time it felt different than what usually came. Not knowing what was about to happen, I became both excited and unnerved. My body began to rise. I felt the bed lose its contact with my backside. As the feeling of weightlessness began to spread throughout my body, I started to feel the ceiling coming closer to my face.

I heard my guides inform me not to be afraid. At the moment I thought my nose was going to touch the ceiling, my spirit was transported to the other side. When my eyes came into focus it was like a welding helmet had been placed over my head. Only seeing through a dimly lit piece of green glass, I quickly scanned the room. I was in a cathedral, a rectangular building. Magnificent stained glass with multi-color shapes replaced the walls and ceilings. Marble pillars spread throughout. Designs depicting events were tiled into the floor. Many people walked to and fro; they appeared as darkly shaped silhouettes. I asked my guides what this place was. They responded by telling me it was one of the staging areas between the transition of life and death. I then felt my body being sent back into my room, just inches above the ceiling. Quicker than I expected, my body was sent bouncing toward the bed.

3

The Teen Years

Becoming accustomed to feeling energies, seeing spirits, and sensing thought patterns of people, I felt that this was what a normal life was. Again I was wrong. I started feeling this pull. I know now it was my higher self forcing me along my next step in the evolution of my mental being. The only way I can describe it was that it was like I had one end of a rope tied to my waist and the other end to a bumper of a car. I had no choice but to run forward or be dragged in the process. This constant urgency began to grow. Still not understanding what it was or where it needed to take me, I knew I had to follow. I was still struggling in the battle between my internal truth and what was told to me by society and religious life. But coming into my own I knew that one of them would eventually dissolve.

Then it began to happen. The first time I remember was once when I woke up to use the bathroom. I walked from one end of the bedroom down the stairs and toward the bathroom, seeing and avoiding all the furniture that was scattered around. Down the flight of steps I headed, toward the opposite side of the hall. I did not realize till I reached the bathroom that not only were the lights off, but my eyes were shut as well. I could see as clearly as if it were in the daytime where every obstacle was. It was as if it were in the afternoon. As soon as I realized this, everything turned to black. This happened many times in the years to come, not only where I lived but also when I went on vacation. And even at times out in nature. This is one talent I wish would have stayed with me in my later years.

If seeing clearly in the dark were the only ability that began to surface, I would have been happy at that. What started next lasted for fifteen years until my understanding of it began to form. Then my perception of it changed. It is a tricky thing to send information from the higher planes and back again. Because we are limited in this physical body as well as in the mental state of who we are, in order to allow us to understand new ideas and concepts, things have to be displayed to us using the images, ideas, and beliefs we each already contain in our minds. My strong background both in this lifetime and in the previous ones had given me a belief system deeply imbedded in heaven and hell. Through this and combined with the ability to sense energy vibrations it became a very trying time for me. I did not know whether I would be visited by archangels or demons. Many a night I trembled with fear not knowing which one would visit. It would always start with the sensing of an upcoming energy shift. Then I would concentrate on it till I understood the energy pattern.

In these appearances at night I would be taken by either party, good or bad, and shown future events. Sometimes it would be on parallel dimensions or realities that exist simultaneously as we are on earth. But at times I became fortunate enough to visit the other side. Those were the experiences I loved the most. I was still trying to struggle to understand what was happening to me and at the same time trying to fit this piece of the puzzle into what I had been taught as right and wrong. Rarely did these pieces even come close to matching the empty areas of life. This in part was one of the pivotal points that allowed me to shift my way of thinking by tossing out what I was taught and allowing the new truth to come in. Of course that took many years down the road and many experiences later.

One of these events I was taken to was sometime in the future. I was standing on a coastal tropical beach. I came to in this place looking up into the sky. I remember standing there and enjoying the rays of sunshine on my body. Looking around I noticed people strolling up and down the beach. Toward my left there were hotels, restaurants, and bungalows. Not knowing where I was, I knew this was somewhere in a foreign land. Then all of a sudden everything went silent—no sounds of birds, no music in the background, and not even the sound of crashing waves. Looking toward the ocean I noticed the water receding. Becoming alarmed I realized then that we were all doomed. Death was shortly upon us. Then I saw it. The biggest tidal wave I ever could have imagined was heading directly toward us. A few seconds later people started to scream and shout. Of course I knew this too was useless.

I used to believe in pre-destiny. It is like creating an outline before writing a term paper, setting up key points that you need to learn prior to arriving upon this earth plane, laid out neatly with all its good and bad trials of life for you to grow and become who you need to be.

After receiving the following vision in my teens, some fifteen years later my theories on pre-destined life came to a shattering halt. My dream started out with me being a supervisor in a manufacturing plant. A new section of building had been erected just a few years prior. In the dream I was hovering about twenty feet off the ground watching myself walking with a new employee, explaining to him what the company did. I watched in the dream as this new employee and I walked into this new building, continued our conversation, turned to the left, and continued to walk away.

Fifteen years passed, and I forgot about this vision. I was working for a company that manufactured pneumatic equipment. At that time I supervised a few employees in the engineering department. A new trainee had joined the department, and as was customary in that situation, I gave them a tour of the plant. I had done this many times with other new co-workers. As I had done many times prior, I explained the details of process we used in building products. As I started walking toward the newly built section of the building, time began to slow down.

My awareness started to shift. It was like I had stepped out of my body and was following these two people and listening into their conversations. Then the vision hit me. I remembered this from years ago in my teens. As if on cue I began quoting what both parties said shortly before they said it. My mind began franticly trying to remember what was next, then there was a memory of me looking down from a twenty-foot height as we walked left when entering into this new section. I was snapped back into my body; I stopped in my tracks, and looking up in front of me I saw a swirling, light colored, misshapen form of my younger self.

Most people would say that this was pre-destiny, but I beg to differ. I was able to stop a part of it by physically stopping myself and staring at my younger self. In the vision I saw both bodies continue walking on their planned course. In reality I was the only one that did not follow this course of action but instead saw myself staring back at me.

Still another time I was guided into the gates of hell, with both of my angels, one on each side of me. This cavernous area was filled with grotesque images of creatures and otherworldly beings. Blood was splattered all over the rocks, and screams echoed off the walls. My guides told me not to be terrified because I would not be harmed. They told me to observe everything. Cutting across the middle of this cavern was a running river. It reminded me of the River Styx. Upon approaching it I noticed that there was more to this river than just the color red. It looked like thick paint. The more I got closer the more I saw that it contained something that appeared to be alive. I moved still closer. This blood-like paint moved on its own. It appeared to contain something under the surface. I watched it move. This living creature rose and sank, repeating these movements back and forth. It reminded me of squirming maggots under a thick coat of paint. I felt the pain and energy under this surface. It felt like multiple individual thoughts. The more I focused on it, the more intense the energy became. I felt this blood river started to increase in strength and life. It suddenly reached out to me. For a split second I thought it would pull me down in its mire. When it got close to my face it recoiled with great force. I realized that this river was not a collection of souls but instead a collection of like-minded thoughts that had coalesced together to transform this creature into a living being.

At first glance one would assume from this terrifying ordeal that hell is a real place. I have to admit it I did think so at one time. But as I underwent other experiences and visions through my life, I began to take another viewpoint of it. In order to create learning experiences, our higher spiritual selves need to take images from our brain. They must find just the right ones that carry the vibration needed to change the subtle shifts in the conscious mind, allowing us to grow and learn to become who we need to be. Having such strong experiences with my religious beliefs as a foundation, I realized that the imagery was not the true message but instead it was the energy signature behind them. This was my first realization of what tonal vibrations were and how what we say and how we say it has a larger impact than just the words do.

This river of hell contained on the surface blood and gore, but looking below the surface I found that it was the energy signature that had created this creature. It took a life of its own, building and feeding upon itself and amplifying its vibration rate to affect all that it can by pulling tonal vibrations to it. With this lesson I also found that the more you fine-tune your tonal vibration rate, the higher and closer you become toward the source of God himself. By the very rate at which you 'sing' you become less and less affected by the slower or lower rate of vibration of other sources. This is why the hidden aspects of this river could not mix with my refined state. It in turn became repelled by it.

One of the most intense visions I had was toward my later years of life as a teen. It started with an overpowering, massive energy shift, one I hadn't felt to this degree before. Light started to appear in my room. I became afraid to open my eyes. I also knew what was happening to me was not a bad thing. The next thing I remember is that I was on the other side with both of my guides, one standing just behind each shoulder. I stood on top of a rolling meadow.

The colors of the flowers, grass, and sky were so vibrant and sharp I never could have imagined anywhere on earth could be like this. There were variations of colors that my eyes had never beheld. The smells of a fresh springtime breeze filled the air. I gazed upon the sky of beautiful pale blue with the whitest, fluffy clouds. I asked my guides were I was. They said I was in a very special place on the other side. They then told me to head toward the rectangular old building in the center of the valley. As I walked to it I felt the grass hit my legs and wondered in amazement that I could feel this.

At one end of the building there appeared an old wooden door. My angels told me that only I could step through and that they had to remain outside. I stepped in. Once inside I was surprised that this building did not have a floor. It was dark topsoil that appeared to contain many nutrients. And the walls were old, worn planks of wood with one-inch gaps. In each gap a white light shone into the interior. I knew that this light was not from the outside but from the energy vibrations of the one I came to see.

Standing at the other end of this building stood an angelic being, one I had never seen to this degree before. As I tried to gaze upon his face, I found I could not. I humbled myself upon the floor in front of him. At first sight I knew who he was; that being was my protector—the one I would call upon for help and protection throughout my life. Feeling his love hitting me with each wave of his thought, I became unsure of myself. I did not understand why me of all people was allowed a visit from him. After what felt like a long time he spoke to me. He told me to stand up and grab the object that lay on top of the table that appeared in front of him.

This table was covered with a fine, white silk cloth. On top of this cloth lay a chrome, polished, stone-encrusted sword. I reluctantly grabbed the handle of this sword. This angel told me to hold it up. As this sword reached past my chest I noticed the spark of blue flame run from the handle down toward the tip of this object. When I held the sword above my head I saw that the blue flames engulfed the metal blade. It transformed the hard chrome into an intense, multi-colored sword with flames of blue. This flame became intense with both light and energy. A blaze on the blade of this blue flame brightened the interior of the room. I was told to continue with the process.

I knew at that moment to raise this sword up to the four corners: north, south, east and west. Each time I did this, my tonal vibration rate and the vibration rate of the sword became harmonized. Both the sword and myself harmonizing our energies into one solid mass, the sword became an extension of myself. We were as one being at this moment in time. I noticed that the energies contained within the flames of the blade had mixed within my tonal vibration and then returned to the sword and amplified the flames of blue. And the flames ignited and grew stronger and brighter. The sound that echoed off the interior walls was the sweetest, most intense thing I had ever experienced up to that point. And only a few things I have experienced since then can compete with it.

4

The Early Twenties

Being absorbed into life's reality, I had this illusion that my own little piece of it would return to normal. Like other people's dreams, I was to head off to college. Get a degree, then a well paying job. Settle down and live a life that every American dreams. Things were finally turning out. I had received a full-ride scholarship into college. I accepted a full-time job in the summer working for one of the major automotive part suppliers. Working twelve-hour days, seven days a week, allowed me to save enough money so when school arrived I would not have to work. I'd be able to use the extra time to dedicate to my studies.

Little did I realize that my higher self had other plans. I started working the day after graduation. This hectic schedule of working all summer long gave me no time to enjoy the fruits of a high school graduation. I needed a vacation. I convinced my best friend that we needed to enjoy a little free time before the hard work began. We decided that we would both quit our jobs three weeks before the college semester started. We loaded our gear into a 1978 Dodge LeBaron and headed off for a fun-filled two weeks of camping and hiking along the lakes of Michigan.

About a week into this trip we both were getting tired of campfire food and wanted some old-fashioned, good down-home cooking: a pizza with all the toppings. Three hours south of the campsite in a small town we patiently waited to turn left into a pizza joint. My buddy decided to put his new cassette player under the seat. Lucky for him he unbuckled his seat belt and leaned down under the dash to put it away. Then I saw it in my rear view mirror. It was a full-sized Mac truck heading right up behind me. The only thing I could do was to see the clock on the dash. It was 10:28 am. Then everything changed in an instant.

Time slowed down. I saw my buddy fly through the air and slam under the dash of the vehicle. Every second that passed seemed like a minute going by. The next thing I knew was I was above the accident, staring down upon this crash in motion, seeing the truck climb up upon the roof of the car. At the same time, both vehicles merged into one, solid mass. I noticed the force of the impact twisted the car in a ninety-degree angle from the trailer. Cars from either direction also began to slide, attempting to stop, hoping to prevent a collision. I felt the urge to look away. I had no desire to see any more. It was then that everything faded to white before my eyes.

I was somewhere that appeared to be a room. Unlike a normal room this had no walls and no ceiling. White, vibrant light was shining everywhere. The waves of love seem to come in every direction. A feeling of being safe and sound permeated my entire being. I did not want to leave. Just then, as though a whip had cracked in the air, I was forced back into my body. The car was still in motion. The right tire of the Mac truck had shifted and slid off the roof, allowing the left tire just inches from the back of my head to move and settle on the front seat between my friend and me. Later, after the accident, we both laughed when we exchanged stories that at the same moment both of our minds saw a huge explosion. Thankfully it never happened. Strangely what did happen was we both found ourselves outside the vehicle about fifteen feet away looking back at the collision still in progress. Both the Mac truck and my car slid another five feet before coming to a full stop. Then I heard the screeching of tires behind me. Turning around, I saw an oncoming vehicle had stopped just a foot from where we were standing. I remember talking to the woman from behind the wheel; she explained we had appeared out of nowhere.

Did Divine action intercede, allowing us to disappear from inside the vehicle then only to reappear outside, safe from harm to be witness to the accident in progress with our own eyes? Or did something happen so fast that it allowed our bodies to somehow get out of the car before the crash ended? I will never be able to explain how it happened. For me it does not matter if getting out of the car was help Divinely sent or if it was a physical flight or fight response. What the event did start was a chain reaction in revaluating my role in life. I found that the promise of college and a well paying job no longer appealed to me. The realization and fortitude to find out who I was and why I was here came to the forefront of my consciousness. Anything else did not matter.

It took me a few years into college to decide I could no longer ignore this pull. I told myself that I would fully commit my life to finding out who I was, what I was, and what my role was in this divine game of life. I knew that I must follow a path that was not only poorly marked, but that had been overgrown by weeds, trees, and brushes. I knew I must follow wherever my higher being wanted me to go. How would I accomplish such a task?

Even to this day I find it very frustrating that I have felt these subtle changes in the energies around me, and still do not know how or where I should proceed. I decided that there were only two concepts up to this time that I felt were the truth. The first half of the foundation base was my belief in Christ, and the second half was the spiritual pull from my higher self. With these two guideposts, I had my foundation to begin my quest on the journey of self-discovery. No matter how far I stretched on my path I could always compare it to the foundation beneath my feet. If it did not fit I would toss it aside.

At the beginning of this journey I told myself I would not limit myself to my religious upbringing and faith, but instead would view as many different types of philosophies, religions, beliefs, and practices as I could. I would take what I felt fit right with my foundation and toss what did not. For the first time in my life I had a purpose, a direction to follow. Little did I realize that this journey would not only take me across some interesting terrain, but it also had me journey through space, time, and multiple realities.

Like everything else, this too started out easily enough. I spent as much time as I could visiting different churches, libraries, old bookstores, and gatherings of like-minded people. I was a sponge, soaking up what I could. It wasn't too long before I began to collide with what I knew and what I was able to obtain. I would hear these concepts and ideas and feel this friction with my very being, knowing that what I was learning was not correct or only had partial truths in it. Knowing I needed to search elsewhere, abruptly I would head off in another direction. Strangely I found myself back at the beginning of my journey. I found myself walking in a giant circle, which only led me back to the beginning.

In order to understand what I didn't know, I first needed to understand what I did know. The answers I sought needed to be pulled within myself. I knew there lay the answers I sought. I worked just enough to support this new lifestyle. I lived very simply. I spent as much time as I could in nature and took trips to retreat houses and monasteries. What I felt and understood all my life as truth needed to expand my mind to understand concepts that were not contained in any books or teachings. I drew upon the remembrances of my past life with Christ as well as his teachings from the other side of the veil. Using his original concepts and ideas of what he taught upon this earth, I was able to expand my limited mental and spiritual state. Leaping from one foundation to another, I stretched my being to understand greater and greater concepts of truths, refining each level of understanding and purifying and adsorbing each new idea I received. Transforming my foundation allowed greater expansion of my mental and spiritual being. I reconnected to the lost Divinity within, bringing my higher being closer to myself.

5

The Second Set of Lessons

The second major shift in understanding tonal vibrations came in an unlikely series of events. I knew at this time you needed to approach meditation and contemplation within the light of the Divine God. I needed to approach it with a purified state of mind, to remove any worldly thoughts and random projections that flashed before my mind, and to set my intent with purity and oneness with the Divine light. Then I could finally use the focus of my mental capabilities to project a beam of thought toward the oneness with God. I would then achieve a unification of mind, body, soul, and spirit within the body of Divine light. Even with all these guidelines in place I had failed to add to this mix an important piece of the recipe for my journey toward my spiritual destination. I realized later that I miscalculated slightly with my intent.

Human beings have always been taught to look externally for guidance. A child looks to their parents for protection. A person looks toward a doctor for their health. A religious person is needed for the one who is seeking spiritual guidance. When I would set up my time for meditation, I had my usual artifacts of religious items. My cross of Christ was no exception. I would focus my intent upon this item, concentrating my thoughts of my understanding of the Divinity upon the sight of the crucifixion.

Over a period of time I noticed that the statue of Christ would start to move. At first only his head would move. Then weeks later, I noticed the rest of his body would start following the movements of his head. It got to a point that the image of him would change from day to day. Thinking to myself that it was a by-product of my imagination, I still became fascinated by it. Was this an illusion my mind had set into motion? Or was I seeing this as it was really was happening? I would never see the body of Christ on the cross move. But when I would glance away from the cross then back again, it would have changed positions. To my amazement other people would start to notice the movement as well. They had all thought I was playing a practical joke on them and was switching crosses each time they came over. Of course I was not about to let them know what they were seeing was a real miracle happening.

I had noticed that there appeared to be a pattern to his movement. One day his head would be up. Other days his head would be down. And still others he would be sagging low upon the cross. What I found was that his position was dependent upon my spiritual struggles at that time. Then I stopped using it as a focal point and noticed years later that the cross had stopped moving.

The second half of this lesson came in a gift from a friend, who gave me a beautiful picture of Christ. I replaced my cross with this photo and focused my intent upon it. It did not take long for the photo of Christ to begin to change. Over time the same image, in a three-dimensional, transparency copy of the photo had overlaid upon the image on the picture. It would push itself up off the front of the photo and mold into a frontal facial likeness of the picture itself—a translucent image of what the photo was, but in a three-dimensional view. The eyes of this three-dimensional image would follow you around the room. At first it was only when I meditated.

Over time this 3D image evolved to a point that it reappeared every time I came into the room. This three-dimensional face would rise up from the picture and watch me as I walked around. Friends of mine would come in and stop in midstream and could not believe that the face had a translucent appearance and lifelike, three-dimensional image. They could not believe that the eyes would move and would follow them around. I continued to use this photo in my daily meditations for some time after that, until the day arrived when a darker, more sinister creature inhabited the three-dimensional image. This once glorified photo of Christ became a vibrating energy more sinister and darker in nature. I was conflicted, thinking it was a representation of Christ but at the same time feeling its lower vibratory energy signature.

I did eventually find the courage to shred this photo, but it took everything I had to do so. In the minutes leading up to the monumental moment of its demise, the creature that inhabited the picture, sensing its destruction, started to relay messages to me. It made its feeble attempts at telling me it had power over me, that whatever it was would lash out and wreak havoc upon me if I followed through with its destruction. Empty threats, I knew, but the feeling of it still took me by surprise. With all the courage I had I shredded its likeness. After that moment I felt at peace once again.

These two experiences early in my life have taught me a couple of major lessons. First of all the intent, the focus in a purified state must be as exact as I can make it. The second lesson I learned is never to focus my intent outwardly but instead draw upon the divine God within each of us. This will allow a more refined, purified intent that contains very little of the person's energy signature.

When I focus my intent outwardly, a subtle shift, which may seem very small in this physical realm, is changed dramatically when reaching beyond the veil. The distortion that the veil has will cause this misguided attempt to miss its intended target by miles. This is a very critical stage in development and must be constantly monitored throughout one's lifetime. The third major lesson I learned is how objects themselves in any type of ceremony would become alive with repeated focused energy sent to it. This can allow all types of creatures to inhabit the object. Continuously focusing your intent on any object will attract different types of entities. These beings will in turn inhabit the object. The directed energy will feed these beings, keeping them alive. They will do anything to keep that flow directed toward them.

6

Turning Silver to Gold

I have always considered myself a logical person. When things come my way that do not fit in the scope of what we consider normal, I first try to prove it scientifically. When these experiences cannot be explained physically then I reach into the realms of spirit.

From my childhood to my late twenties. I could never wear jewelry and watches. Even the high-priced stainless steel pieces would have the same effect on my personal being. If it was a metal watch, I could drain its batteries within days. Or I could get the hour or minute hand to swirl around the dial. Nothing would ever keep time, always running much faster than a normal watch would. The only watches I could wear were the heavy plastic watches, and even those would only last for five to six months before the batteries would drain. This was including new batteries being replaced when the old ones wore out. Rings and necklaces were also a problem. I would leach the metal right out of them. Wearing jewelry would stain my skin in the same location as items were placed. More expensive pieces and even stainless steel would still cause the same result.

So to my surprise, in my mid-twenties I accepted three medallions from friends. One was a stainless steel cross. The second one was the icon of Padre Pio. The third one was a metal cross with the body of Christ on it. Even though I had never wanted to wear jewelry, I was strangely attracted to wearing these. I went out and purchased a high-quality stainless steel necklace to bear the weight of these medallions.

I wore these pieces all the time, both in my waking and sleeping state. I washed them with soap and water a couple of times a week. Within months of wearing them I noticed changes appearing on the surface on these medallions and on the necklace. They were subtle at first but began to gain momentum in these changes. What eventually happened was that the raised edges on the metal cross started to become gold-like in appearance.

This spread through the entire piece until approximately eighty percent of it was covered. Both sides were affected. The second piece, Padre Pio, had turned one hundred percent blood-red. And the third piece, the cross with Christ, had first turned gold on the back. The nail holes shown also on the back had turned blood-red. On the front the image of Christ was golden, and the surface of the cross turned blood-red. This medallion was the only one that changed again and again over time. The image of Christ would first cover itself in a blood-red stain. Then it would switch to a golden color, then to black. Then back to blood red. This happened multiple times. The stainless steel chain started to change as well. Every third link turned golden in appearance. This was in a time of my spiritual evolution where great strides were taking place. Many things were opening up and revealing themselves to me.

My first thought was that each surface had a stainless steel appearance and underneath it were the multiple layers of other colors. By wearing these pieces you would eventually remove the outer surface, and the surface underneath would be shown.

Luckily the company I worked for at the time had a high-powered magnifier. Under this machine I noticed that the gold, bloodstain, and black stain were layers that had been added on top of each surface. The changes that appeared on these pieces were added to the surface in multiple layers. Years later I stopped wearing them and noticed that most of these changes had disappeared. What was left had changed to a duller shine. They still retain some of the gold, blood red, and black in places. Other people have seen these and also could not believe these changes had occurred.

7

A Visit from an Angelic Being

Everyone has epic tragedies in their lives, and I was no exception. One of these types of events happened in my twenties. I cannot pinpoint it as one major event, but rather a couple of smaller episodes that happened in quick session. The result of this sent me into an uncontrollable sorrow. I can remember that evening as if it were yesterday. I broke down in tears and sobbed. Crying alone is not in my nature, but this night everything seem to line up and hit me like a ton of bricks. I can remember pleading to my angels and God, why did this happen? What did I do or not do to have caused this? I felt I had no one to turn to.

I desperately needed a shoulder to lean on. The pain from this event not only caused deep sorrow in my heart but also sent my mind into despair. My body felt anguished. Physical pain I felt. Joints stiffened, my muscles felt complete exhaustion, and the heart felt like it was breaking. I blamed myself, how could I let it happen? Why couldn't I be more giving? The answers never came. Most of all I felt that I had all these unique abilities I could call up and use, but none of it was any good. I fell asleep that night hoping and wanting to return home to the other side. I hoped God would have the compassion to grant me the wish to not wake up. I felt that I did not want to continue life anymore.

I was always a person who slept on my back. Sleeping on my stomach always caused me discomfort. This night was different. The next thing I remember is waking up on my stomach with my head facing the direction of the wall. I had felt like I had just come out of a deep, cocoon-type of slumber—a sleep that gave me the impression I had been out for days. I lay there remembering the events of the previous day, staring into the blackness of my bedroom. It felt like minutes had gone by. Suddenly I noticed a reflection of light emitting from behind me and bouncing off the wall.

This light grew in intensity and volume till the whole room lit up as if a floodlight had been placed in the center. I started to pick up my head and turn around to see what was happening and just then an angelic, female voice spoke to me. She had told me not to look back but instead to just lie there and enjoy it. I felt the bed shift as if someone had come up and sat down on it next to me. Then a hand was placed upon the midsection of my back. This hand never moved but had been lovingly put there. Then things started to change. I sensed the loving, healing energy that was emitting from this heavenly sent angel. Wave after wave of love was being sent to me.

I noticed that each wave I felt was made up of three components. The first component was the Divine love in the light that shined and filled the entire room. The second was the loving vibration wave that this heavenly angel was sending out, and the last was the tonal sound that emitted from not only her touch but also her sweet voice. The more aware I became, the brighter the room was and the more loving the experience was. In concert with each other, the combination of the light, the loving wave, and the tonal sound being emitted broke the sadness in my heart.

All at once, it was like a dam breaking, sending large volumes of water downstream. With its healing water, it was washing away the sorrow. Her love and kindness replaced and healed the deep scars I had placed upon my interior self. I sat there for the first time, and in some ways the only time, in complete love, tenderness, compassion, and contentment with everything and everyone. Oh, how I miss that. For I wished it would have lasted forever. I felt like a child who was wrapped up in his mother's arms without a care in the world. I fell asleep with total peace. As you can understand, that was the best sleep of my life.

I woke up the next morning later than usual. To my amazement I felt totally refreshed. I remembered one hundred percent of what had transpired both from the day before and what had happen the previous night. My pain was gone. The events that happened twenty-four hours before no longer had the same effect on me. I moved around the house like I was fifty pounds lighter. Joy filled my heart. I will never be able to fully explain the closeness and love that this heavenly angel had given me. Interestingly enough, every object in that room radiated with the energies of the night before. I did not want to leave it. Just feeling it brought back the intense experience. I was forever changed. I even felt different. This level of intense love remained in not only in my bedroom but also in myself for weeks afterward.

8

The Transformation: Switching Realities

During most of my twenties, I experienced major growths in my spiritual development. I would have never believed the things that had transpired within that time frame if I had not lived it myself. These changes were not so much a physical thing. They impacted me in other ways. I achieved major strides in the mental, spiritual, and multi-dimensional shifts. My mind stretched into abstract concepts. Thoughts became theories. And theories became facts in my universe. These new abstract concepts and Divine laws became the new foundation under my feet. Doors began opening up. I felt as though I were an explorer sent into a one-thousand-room mansion and was told to freely roam. I learned to understand energy shifts and how they changed each level of thought. Through each change in a thought wave, the energy of the world changed. I discovered that there were many different types of realities that existed in parallel with the physical life on earth.

The more I learned about these miracles, the more I became consumed by it and the more time I spent pursuing it. I became more comfortable in this altered state than in the physical reality in which I was living. At first I could only achieve these states of awareness while meditating. Over time this had changed. Throughout the day while awake I developed an ability to split my mind into two independent streams of thought. I then could pull both realities into one and work with them side by side.

I found that during this process, I walked in this world with very little interaction with people. It was as if I were invisible to them. I know I did not actually disappear, but for some reason I would be off their radar. I would walk into a crowded room, and nobody would know I was there. Physical touch happened less and less until it stopped altogether. A pat on the back, a shake of the hand, and even a simple hug became nonexistent. Of course there was a reason for this. When part of my mind was heavily into my other reality, my energy would change.

I had to be careful not to touch anyone. Electricity surges would leap from my body and shock the person I was with. It was not like a static shock that you get from rubbing your feet upon a carpeted floor. But the energy exchanged upon touching someone would send a jolt toward the unlucky recipient. This would normally send that person a few steps back. They would look at me with eyes widen, staring at me in disbelief. I spent years with no physical contact with others. I convinced myself it was a by-product of my spiritual self-discovery.

Even while all this was going on, I was still getting visits from my angels and my guides almost on a nightly basis. Although I felt more comfortable and relaxed in what was happening, I still questioned why these events were happening to me. At first, I foolishly tried to tell my family and friends about it. Soon I realized that was a mistake. It is one thing when you're standing on solid ground and then allow the winds of others to hit you. It is another when you're standing on shifting sand and allow others to express their concerns. This taught me that my spiritual journey was a one-person path. I could not at that time take another along for the ride.

Off alone I went. Some people told me that I was mentally unstable. Still others explained to me that the path I was following was heading me straight to hell. They would say I was possessed and needed saving. I chuckled to myself when I would hear it from them. I truly felt sorry for them. I knew what I was going through was divinely sent. I also knew that hell did not exist. Hell was only a concept in the minds of people who gave into that form of faith. A belief in the traditional hell helped them, but it wasn't for me. I had to see this through. I had to keep up the momentum of this change. I did not know where it was going but was excited to find out.

The things I learned were amazing: energy shifts and wave patterns; how everything in this reality was a collection of energy waves. Living things like dogs, trees, and rocks emitted a tonal vibration outward. I learned how the consciousness of a dog compared to a tree and a person were different, but they all still contained aspects of each other. I don't believe in the evolution of a soul from a plant to a bug, to an animal then to a person. I do believe that each living thing emits a living spark of the Divine. It rushes out as each wave of energy of thought hits the atmosphere. As I began to grow, my understanding of these energies that were within each thought began to deepen. I learned how these energy waves of thought would change and influence other thoughts. This was not mind control, but when used in the proper context it was the connection of my divinity within to the divinity of an another. Whether it was a tree, dog, or a person, it did not matter. All responded accordingly.

Then a major breakthrough occurred: I found the connection needed to influence the energy within all things that were in this world by affecting the vibration rate, the tonal energy signature, and the energy waves. I have to admit that at first I wasn't using this newfound talent for the noblest of intents. I experimented with simple things like streetlights. I was able to change them during a three-month period so I would not have to stop at a red light. My friends would comment on occasion, when they were in my vehicle, that we never hit a red light. I then tried these experimentations on dogs. If enough focus was directed toward an animal, I could stop a dog in its tracks. They would turn their head toward me and tilt it to one side then to another. I gave them little commands to bring me their favorite toy, sit next to me, or go to someone; within seconds they would accomplish the task I sent them out to do.

After months of playing with this new talent I came to the realization that I was using the applications incorrectly. This gift, I learned, was used to re-link things in life back to their Divine selves. To forcefully influence others did neither them nor me good. There were lessons they came into life to experience, and those lessons needed to be lived. It was wrong for me to remove those lessons by changing or shifting the energy signatures of others. When this came to the forefront of my conscious thought, my pursuit changed into a new set of rules, guidelines, and paths.

9

The Training as a Healer

There are many different types of healing modalities out there—traditional western medicine, eastern techniques, and spiritualist hands-on healing just to name a few. My individualized way of healing did not come from these traditional, worldly taught ways. I did not attend any seminars or a college of learning to develop this talent.

My abilities came from in part from me remembering what I had developed in past lives along with what I had taught to others on the other side of the veil. At first the major hurdle was the frustration I felt knowing these things but not being able to put them into practice. It was like being an overage, out-of-shape athlete who at some time in their earlier life had set world records but later in life could not even come close to their earlier achievements. I was no different.

Then I started to connect what seemed to be independent ideas into a working prototype. I took what I was learning about the tonal vibrations, along with the energy signatures and the healing modalities, wrapped them up, and merged them in with the Divine intent. With this combination I was able to break through the thick veil of thought and concept and bring these energies forth into the physical reality. This is where it got interesting.

When I began to learn new theories that formed within my metal and spiritual being, I always tried to compare them with my foundation. I needed something to feel safe with, for many concepts and directions were continuously pounding within my conscious mind. I needed a sounding board of sorts. These new ideas were no different. And it felt right. The concept when completed gave a tonal vibration of its own, and it had a sweet sound to it.

I started simple at first: putting my hand on someone's shoulder, adding healing energies to a spoken sentence. I have eventually fine-tuned it to be able to radiate from my being when I walk into a room. Many times these people felt good and relaxed. They would feel this peace for days afterward. I did not attempt to heal them physically or mentally but instead gave them a link to their own Divine self. I simply facilitated their journey to discover their connection themselves. I have gone into places and calmed dying people without a word being spoken. When I did lay my hands in prayer to heal, people felt sparks of energy being transferred from myself to them. I have removed headaches and pain, lessened sorrow, and lifted spirits of individuals. I have even on occasion, as reported by the individuals, levitated them slightly off their chair when healing.

I don't want you to think I can manifest things out of thin air. It is not because of my lack of trying, but rather that it contradicts the spirit of the laws I have formed in the healing practices. It would be incorrect to say I can manifest and grow lost limbs or make a person walk. What I am trying to say is I have been able to shift a person's mental state so they themselves could make the connection on some level to their own cosmic self. I helped reconnect them back to the Divine and pull it through this thick veil into the physical reality on earth. I have repeatedly, though later in life not consistently, rewired someone's connection so successfully that they themselves would contact me weeks later and explain the events that happened after I had met them. Each story I heard was similar in nature. They all felt years younger. Their pains, both mental and physical, disappeared. They felt that they had floated around their daily lives for days on end. People who had been tired would report that they had an overabundance of energy and slept very little. Some said they started doing things that they once loved but had stopped doing in their later years. They all wanted to know if I could bottle it and sell it.

These healing abilities I developed came about through hard work, sweat, and many years of practice. Most of it was removed from me by an event in my thirties, which I will cover later in this book. It took me eight years of hard work to be able to regain and practice a small portion of what I was able to do in my twenties. I can still call upon it in the present time, but I am no longer able to consistently bring it through the veil one hundred percent of the time. I had to rebuild and re-establish these links differently. There are periods of time when I cannot draw upon it. Generally I would only achieve a smaller portion of it.

I know it is hard for you to believe in what I have told you. It sounds like something out of a science fiction novel. I have to admit there have been times where I myself find it hard to believe. If it weren't for the accounts of others giving me feedback, I don't think I would have been able to continue with it. We're dealing with energies that cannot be seen by most people. A lot of the work I do in this field cannot be seen, heard, or felt using the five senses. The results from it can, however, and sometimes it takes the outcome to gauge the process. When you consider the desired results you can in turn change the steps needed to reach the end result.

10

A Major Lesson on Healing With Intent

From the experiences I gained up to this point in my life, I knew I needed to be careful in how I approached the development of these spiritual gifts. The healing aspect was no different. I needed to have a pure intent and to strip as many non-essentials of my lower self and re-link my higher, Divine self with my conscious mind. Unlike most healing practitioners, I did not subscribe to the belief that one must lose one's lower self, one's personality, in order to heal. I did not believe that it was totally God himself that did the one hundred percent of the healing. Instead I approached it as a joint effort. With the merging of all three, my conscious self, my divine self, and the Divine God. I felt they were all pieces in a puzzle. Unless all three pieces combined, I could not have a complete, finalized image. However, I had overlooked a crucial piece: the intent and process were correct, but the alignment was off.

When I healed through the spoken word, a thought, or laying of hands, I forgot one important puzzle piece. When I transferred this connection to another, a large piece of my tonal energy went with it. On the surface it may not seem like much, but it was. It took me weeks and sometimes months of preparation in meditation, contemplation, and prayer to raise my tonal vibrations to a state where I could affect others. In the transfer, most of the energy would be transferred to the person I was healing. This was good for them. They felt wonderful things and moved around their lives for weeks feeling the best they had in years. Because a piece of me was mixed with their energies, I felt like I was living two lives simultaneously. I felt like I was myself and at the same time the person sharing the experiences after they received the healing. I would know what they were doing, their state of mind, and whether they felt pain. I would ask them weeks later if they had done these tasks at different times during the week and what their mood was. I would explain what they were thinking through the week. They could not believe what I was saying, for it was true.

I constantly felt the drain of energy being sent from me to the person I had healed. I tried at first to reestablish the Divine connection, but I was not able to pull energies through as fast as it was going out to those people. It took me some time, but I developed a way to disconnect them so I would not be weakened too much from it. I would document the day and time when I did this and then ask them when they felt that the high they had received diminish. They all said it stopped strangely the same time as I was disconnecting them from myself.

Even with the ability to disconnect others so the drain of energy was not too intense, I found it wasn't enough. I knew deep down I had the answer, but I could not bring it to the forefront of my mind. It became an illusive shadow I could glimpse out of the corner of my eye. I would sense it and turn quickly to look upon it, and it would then suddenly disappear. When it finally decided to show itself, I could not believe how simple it was. I had to slightly adjust my intent; instead of sending the Divine light through my connection, I needed to make a carbon copy of it and lay it upon the person I was healing. Once this was done I had to reconnect the strands from their lower self to their divine self. It took me some months to correctly accomplish this, but when it finally came into focus the draining of my energy stopped.

One of the misconceptions in healing, and I have heard it many times, is that if a person does not want to be healed you cannot heal them. This never felt right with me. If you look at the intent of these people and how they heal others, they are correct in saying that. When I compared the same idea to my healing modality, I realized quickly that it wasn't true. First of all, you are not approaching the person with the intent to heal them physically, mentally, or spiritually. By doing so you strip them of their own Divine right to their own experiences. Secondly, you're taking partial ownership in the creation process. You're accepting the Divine God within you. Accepting the Divinity within the Divine God is not making you a god separate for the Divine godhead. Instead, by accepting your Divinity, you're giving back to yourself what God has already given you. You then move from a state of a child and parent relationship to a co-partnership. You need all the pieces in place in order for this machine to work correctly. I like to refer to it as the next step in our evolution of higher consciousness.

The other aspect in healing is that the main intent is to reestablish the Divine connection. The goal is to allow the person being healed to have a respite from their trials. Then they are able to let their Divine self make the decision about whether to heal or to endure for the lessons they have to learn. When I came across someone who did not want a healing, but who had asked me for it, I would see a wall blocking between us. You don't break it down, as some people might suggest. You realize that the vibrations that you're tapping into are at a higher rate than the one you're healing. You can easily slip through the wall, as if it did not exist, just the same way a ghost would.

11

Let There Be Coin

Always running events logically in my mind, I had at first dismissed these occurrences of coins appearing around my house to holes in my pockets. I'd dealt with seeing coins appear and scatter everywhere all my life. These coins were never larger than quarters and mostly were pennies, nickels, and dimes. I never paid much attention to it. I had heard stories that spirits drops coins to show that they are still alive.

At that time I did not totally believe in it, though I always thought it interesting when someone would tell me a story on the subject. I always told myself I had to be more careful and to make sure I didn't drop them. Never finding any holes, rips, or tears in my pockets, I then chalked it up to the coins working themselves out of my pants and onto the floor. If I did not pick them up, new ones would not appear.

When I would pick them up, days later new ones would take their place. I always wondered why my coin jar never got bigger. I would laughingly tell my angels that they should be dropping bigger denominations like twenty-dollar bills. That never happened.

Then a series of events changed my mind. The first one was when I was on the phone. I was walking past my kitchen table into the living room when about ten feet from me a flicker of light appeared, approximately three feet above the floor. I quickly recognized a round, glittering shape flickering in mid-air. It spun in a backward spinning motion before hitting the floor. It bounced off the floor and, still spinning, arced toward me and landed on my sock. Looking down, I noticed a new, clean quarter lying on my foot. I stood there in amazement trying to rationalize it.

First I glanced around the room to see if it had fallen off something but came to a quick conclusion that there was nothing near it to have fallen off of. Then I thought somehow it had either been on my foot or under it and that I'd picked it up when walking. This did not seem logical because of the direction of the spin on the coin and the arc it made toward me. I thought it interesting but paid little attention to it.

The second time I was again on the phone. This time I was sitting, and I noticed another flash. About eight feet from me, something materialized out of thin air, hung for about what seemed like two seconds, and then dropped with a thud onto the floor. It fell in the middle of a hallway, which was light and bright at the time. There were no doorways it could have bounced through or furniture that it could have fallen off of. Recognizing it as from a spirit, I did acknowledge them and then apologized for not believing them earlier. I then said, "Send me something bigger next time."

About three weeks later I was sitting in the same chair on the phone again, talking to the same person. I noticed in the same location a black object appeared out of nowhere and floated to the ground. Walking up to it I saw it was a crumpled up piece of lint about two inches in diameter. I told them that I thought their joke was funny.

The dropping of the coins in some ways really tore at me in two directions. I had my logical mind saying there had to be a rational explanation. The spiritual side of myself kept saying what more proof of life after death do you want? As small as it appears in comparison to the other magnificent events that happened prior to and after this event, this one could be explained both ways. Logically, the dropped coins could be the result of my hands pushing the coins out when grabbing my keys.

Some of them also could be attributed to holes in the pockets even though I rarely have them. You could even stretch the imagination by saying the dropping of the coins was due to a reflection hitting the pupils of my eyes. My mind, desperately trying to formulate an acceptable answer in what I had seen, came up with what my mind was able to accept. But I know what I saw. It was no different seeing these things manifesting out of thin air as it was seeing someone across from me at a kitchen table.

I do believe these droppings of coins came from spirit. Over time my mind started playing tricks on me, and my mind began to hop over the fence from one side to the other. Then only moments later returning to its original position. My mind kept telling me that I needed to believe in what the five senses perceived, and yet it saw an event that it could not explain.

The things I have noticed in any of the events that happened in my life, is that at the time it's going on, I knew without a doubt that what I was experiencing was Divinely sent. And for a while I stayed steadfast in my belief. But time changes your mind. You start to settle back into the old ways of thinking, dealing with the five senses. Its not that your faith is shaken but the logical mind starts to question these events.

Your mind begins to question your memories in life all over again. It tries to tell you that it never happened, or if you did really experience it, then make it happen again, now. I wish I could repeat a lot of the events that I experience, but sadly it doesn't work that way. I have no proof about what happened, but I do know that I will experience other things in my future. This helps me reestablish the foundation in my belief structure.

I had to come back to this chapter to let you know an additional point. I have experienced coins appearing around my house all my life. In the last ten years it has amplified three-fold. It came to a point that I would not pick up them because I knew spirit would just replace them again in a few days. What had changed abruptly in the months that had passed since writing this chapter is that the coins suddenly stopped appearing. This became another confirmation that what I had experienced throughout my life was not my imagination but instead spirit-sent.

12

Departed Souls, Spirits, Angels, and High-level Beings

It's no secret that a spirit occasionally appears alongside my bed at night. I also have the ability to sense different spirits, both ones that have passed and also ones that have come from a dimension that resides along this earth but that is not from it. Everyone and everything vibrates at a unique level. Our tonal vibrations are like fingerprints: no two are alike. You can blend two spirits' energies together, and they form a new energy signature. Spirits on the other side and in other dimensional states are no different. Their energy signatures are different than our own. This is largely due to the vibration needed to maintain the reality from were they come. What does happen is that they feel totally different than us. This is one reason that people become terrified when feeling these beings approach. When I look closer into every being in all these realms they share a common energy signature. It is subtle, but it is used to link our souls all together.

The multi-dimensional spirits, for a lack of a better term, do not exhibit the vibration rate that is only associated with conscious minds that have lived on this planet. They have a personality, but it did not develop from living on earth. They have a very interesting energy signature. I know only of one reality where the energies can be joined and form a physical manifestation.

This plane we live in is largely influenced by our physical surroundings. The other realities are not like this, at least the ones I have seen. There, matter is made up of pure thought. A collective mass of thought produces a manifestation of their surroundings. I like to attribute energy to a sampling of both this world and the other realm we call heaven. These beings are more spiritually advanced then we are.

They see the connection that we all share. They feel that Divine God connection within each of us. They are similar in nature to the physical race. Like us on this physical realm, we all contain different strengths and weakness. They are no different in nature. The only major difference I can tell is that because they can communicate with their Divine connection more easily, evil does not exist on that side as it does in this physical reality. They know that every impact good or bad has an effect in their own realm. This is one major reason they attempt to help the best way they can in our own physical reality.

I have on occasion been visited by what I call the dons of the universe. These beings are so highly developed that their energies are not one hundred percent compatible with our own. They are a collective group of spirits that make sure the development of universes proceed along the path of what the Divine God has intended it to. They normally only take a wide view of things and let the lower highly developed spirits manage the details in each planet's development. These beings are not among what we call the order of angels the way archangels are. The dons are in a class of their own. Each spirit is made up of a collection of like-minded spirits that have merged themselves together to create a collective whole. They only come closer to individual realms when great change is being made. Dons take a more active role in ensuring that critical steps are made to accomplish a desired task. They allow the members of the order of angels to handle the details of these changes.

These dons of the universe are very intense and strong, and they have an extremely unusual energy signature. When they visit, I shake from their presence. They do not have a conscious personality mindset like humans do, and they feel different from otherworldly visitors. I can take almost every type of energy signature there is. I have been humbled, exalted, and supercharged by many spirits' tonal vibrations. The dons are the only beings to date that are so intense that I find it hard at times to absorb what I am feeling. Major changes in myself are generally a direct result of their visits. I have had energy surges before. These are not like that.

Massive energy shifts have happened since 1996, especially starting in the year 2000 and for many years after that. These high-level beings are coming closer to this planet to take a more hands-on approach. They are interceding in this realm when critical changes are made.

Instability always arises when an energy expansion is made. They have to be very careful in coming too close to this reality because of the incompatibility with their tonal vibrations and ours. The problem is not that their energies would destroy but the terror we individuals would feel because of the alien nature of their tonal vibrations. When we are most suited to handle their energies, they approach. They are terrifying in the same way watching a horror show can be terrifying. Yet, they project the feeling of love. I do shake in their presence.

13

The Late Twenties

With each step I took along my path of enlightenment I became more and more graceful and sure-footed. I developed a stronger and greater confidence in myself. As crazy, unusual, and spiritual as my life became, there was always this underlying foundation of grace and peace. I was like a willow tree. As the torrents of rain and wind bent every branch and moved every leaf, my roots remained firmly entrenched in the rich, nutrient-based soil.

I became stronger and filled with a deep sense of richness as each moment passed. This newfound passion in understanding my true self and how I fit into God's reality only took a stronger hold on my reality. I no longer desired the physical life and all its gifts. Its effects and lures no longer had a hold on me as it once had. My ideas of what I wanted in life started to change. As months turned into years, the physical life and all it had to offer became a less of an importance to me till they eventually became merely a means to survive.

These things no longer interested me, and they became a means to an end as breathing, water, or shelter had for one's survival. I began to spend as much time as I could by surrounding myself with the visual stimulation of monasteries, retreat houses and nature. These new surroundings became my new teacher. My thirst for truth was my consuming flame. It spread throughout my body till it consumed my every thought. I did work in those years.

To survive in this physical reality you have to support yourself. It was just enough to support this newfound passion. I did not need any social life. I did not care to obtain friends and a family. My focus was to learn about truths and concepts of the Divine, then to implement those newfound rules in practical ways. To see the effects it would have upon this physical plane would allow me the confirmation that what I was doing had not only a purpose but a tangible one as well.

Life for me at that time had changed. I was stretching my reality and my mental state to a point beyond what I thought could be imagined. I did a lot of things in secrecy. No one knew exactly the extent and wholeness of the things I was accomplishing then. I desired nothing but the constant presence of the Divine within and around me. I wanted only to feel the love, strength, grace, and power constantly pulsating through my being. I was beginning to understand concepts, ideas, and realities that existed beyond what our mind can perceive. These things only sweetened and enhanced the constant state of euphoria I was in.

As if a bomb had exploded within my brain, an idea had formed. The accumulation of all these spiritual ideas and concepts I had experienced up to this point filled my mind, compressing, merging and combining until it had no other place to go but to spill out into my consciousness. I realized at this moment that I desired nothing less than the total immersion within this newfound world.

I was not trying to escape this physical world by any means. There was no major catastrophe that caused me to want to run from reality. Instead I felt I was being constantly pulled by my higher self to experience more of this altered state of reality. Admittedly, I was addicted to it. I constantly craved it. I yearned for every moment of my life to be centered upon this newfound truth I had discovered. Eating, sleeping, working, and living in this reality became a burden.

This physical reality was a thorn stuck under my fingernail. In my heightened state I became more aware of the energies of these high-level beings that surrounded me. I felt like I was part of a large, close-knit group of majestic spirits that had surrounded me and never left. They became my new family. They were more than just my angels and guides; they were my companions upon this journey of life.

I was seeing everything with new eyes. I came to the realization that up to this point in my life I was living an illusion and I had been blind to this newfound reality. For the first time in my life I could visualize the richness and fullness of everything. My visual stimulation had changed. I could perceive what everyone else could, but I could now also take that image and overlay what my spiritual mind's eye had visualized.

The best way I can explain what I saw is that it was as if I had two separate transparencies of the same image except, each one having slightly different things in them. Using both images I could then begin to acquire a complete photo. It was also like a camera capturing two images on one negative, with the first image showing the physical realm and the second photo showing the energies and movements in the first. Watching the spectrum of colors and intensity of each rainbow of waves of vibrating energy emitting from every living thing astounded me.

I sat for hours amazed by what I saw and felt. I felt each wave pulsating out from the center and spread in all directions outward. I watched it interact with other energy tides, felt the interaction of each energy wave when it hit another incoming wave, saw these two energies both combining and deflecting at the same time. Then a piece of this energy would mix, and in an altered form would be sent back along the ripple toward where it had come from. I found this fascinating and became truly amazed by it.

Those pieces of the original wave that had been sent out combined with other incoming waves; mixing parts of all energy signatures, they catapulted themselves back upon themselves until they hit the creator of that wave. This returning wave would then interact once again with its creator. The tonal vibration of the living being that created it would be slightly changed. The interaction of each vibrating wave when mixed together with others and then having pieces of it returning to its creator had different impacts depending on what the original source was. Stronger and weaker signals were largely due to the type of collision of the other wave. Waves from animals, human beings, and plants all felt different. It was amazing to see how we as individuals are interlinked to everything around us. The illusion of reality that each one of us creates, then binds the changes of our being to it.

Then it happened. This physical world became a dream. That truth which I desired so much became my reality. Time changed in it. My surroundings slowed down—and in some cases stopped entirely. Abstract concepts came to me easily. Understanding depths of things clearly was as easy as remembering how to tie a shoe. As my concept of reality broke down, I became both alarmed and excited about it. Taking this giant leap was terrifying. The accepted "truth" of what we see, hear, and believe became only a shadow compared to what was being given to me.

My mind struggled with this battle, trying to send me back to what I knew was reality and at the same time dragging me along to what I was becoming. The veil that separates us from our own Divine self and the Divine God became extremely thin. My mind stretched to its limits. One side was still attached to this world, and the other part of my mind was rooted in this new reality of truth and my consciousness. I felt my sanity was in the middle trying to grasp at both ends. With no one to turn to, to give me an answer of what was happening to me, I started to get scared. *Am I losing my mind?* I thought. That was quickly shaken off. I knew I was not crazy, even though on the surface it appeared to be true from someone else's perspective.

I knew what I was experiencing was as real as sitting here telling my life story. Should I totally give in and see where this journey would lead? Could I toss my family aside, like a discarded item that was no longer wanted? Is that what I needed to do? All these and other questions ran through my mind. I knew at that moment that I could drop all those worldly things. As much as I loved them, I could leave them behind. There was much to be learned in this new world. There was much to be experienced in it.

I decided at this moment to dedicate my life completely to this new reality. I decided to spend one last week at a monastery I was attending before telling them I wanted to join. To leave my old life behind and begin a new one in contemplation and reflection was my new objective. It wasn't till a couple of days before the end of this week when I started to feel something coming. So I focused my intent upon it.

First it became a feeling, then it grew into a vision of a sequence of events in the future. In my childhood and far into my young adult life I had always seen and felt this woman, that one whom I thought at that time was the one I would marry. I saw the way her hair flowed around her head and over her shoulders, the way she moved, filled with grace in every stride. I sensed the waves of love from her gaze and felt her touch, her gentle pressure upon my arm and shoulder. Her tender voice was as sweet as honey to my ears. I was shown a life with her, the marriage life we would have, the children that would be born. I saw the joy and love I would feel toward my wife and kids.

I watched each child experience and learn things for the first time. Then I watched our lives as we grew old together. For the first time in my life I felt the loneliness of not having a family. I felt the joy of living a life shared with others. My yearning for it grew and grew till it consumed my every thought. I wanted this life I saw. I felt it had been denied me for so long, and I demanded it. I did not want another life like so many of the previous ones I had lived before. Serving a greater purpose and losing my own personal desires in the process was not going to be an option in this life. I was going to make sure that this did not happen again.

I decided at the end of the stay to decline the monk's life, and I kindly told them I would not be joining. I knew then I had to live in this reality if I ever wanted the life that was shown to me. Life throws you curve balls. You look at all the things that someone could experience that would not only stop them in their tracks but turn their views one hundred eighty degrees around on the spot—I would never have thought it would be the visions of a life with someone I loved.

I decided to drop my journey and only deal with what my five senses could perceive. I felt at that time I could only deal with one reality and to keep my sanity I would choose what everyone else has done. I find myself looking back on this experience, which seem a lifetime ago, as a cruel joke. Those visions changed my life drastically and onto a new set of learning. But they never did happen. Images still burned in my brain are so vivid, so real, and yet they never manifested. At least that is what I believed till the eventful day many years later. But you will have to wait till the end of this book to see what happened.

I ended my journey. I told myself that working hard in life, buying a home, and saving for retirement is what I needed. I told myself that living a simple life would be no longer. I was going to live comfortably and prepare for the arrival of the woman in the vision. Dropping my spiritual quest, I went bravely toward my new life, not realizing that the spiritual journey would not leave me. It sent reminders to me. Stronger and stronger they became, till I could no longer ignore it.

14

My Denial and the Major Decision

I gave in to public pressure. I decided to work hard and prepare for this new life that I felt I was denied for so long. Dealing with the spiritual aspect of life is a hard one. You deal with ideas and concepts that take a long time to perceive and formulate. After months and months of effort a theory forms.

Then when the theory becomes solidified, you need to in turn run it through its paces again and again to prove or disprove these abstract concepts. And after all that you have a foundation that fits within your belief structure. Even when all is said and done, this newfound system still has a hard time coming forth into the reality of the five senses. It is not as easy as looking over your shoulder and seeing the manifestations of this worldly life—people around you, a sidewalk under your feet as you stride on by.

When you take spiritual jumps, you have to go beyond the ability to perceive it by faith alone. You need to exercise these ideas to make them mold more into your daily life. This is not an easy task by itself. It is much easier to set your goals upon the concrete things like a family, home, a nice car, and a job and to allow these to manifest into your life.

I started to work longer hours at my current job, putting in sixty-five to eighty hours a week. I worked non-stop like this every day for months at a time. I kept telling myself I would prove my worth and see the fruits of my labor. I started a business of my own on the side doing many different things like photography, building computers, and drafting. Between both jobs I usually only slept four to five hours a night.

My spiritual side never left, but instead I kept pushing it deeper and deeper within myself. And when it did rise to the surface I reminded myself that it took too much energy and time to maintain only a fraction of what was there. I reminded my being that it was much easier to live in the moment. Be like everyone else, I kept telling myself.

A few years passed, and I had collected what I considered a nice nest egg. The yearning for the spiritual life kept on finding ways to tell me that I was happier in that path than the one I was now following. My dream of traveling around the United States started to surface again. I had always wanted to move from town to town and help when I was needed, to help along the way, and then to move to another town or state when the work was completed.

A part of myself said I finally had enough money to follow this dream. My other side said differently. I told myself, you have insurance, and good job and a nice life, why would you want to toss it aside for something you cannot put the five senses around? What I felt was logic at that time won out. I decided to take the safer route. I convinced myself that I needed a grounding foundation, a major change, to force me not to choose the other lifestyle, so I bought a house.

This house was, in some ways, was a long-time dream—to find a place that needed fixing up, then follow the American dream and become a handyman. I was fortunate in my earlier years to have a father who had taught me many things about house repair. I felt comfortable doing these things, so I took my life savings and found a house that had what looked like eighteen years of neglect. This house was on a corner lot and was nineteen hundred and fifty square feet.

In the back yard I had a in-ground swimming pool that was built in the seventies. This house even had a room with a wet bar and a fireplace for those days when I wanted to have a pool party. I realized from the start this place had been neglected. However, I did not realize the extent to which this place needed repairs.

I should have sat down and added together what each repair would have had cost. I would have realized that purchasing a house that was already completed would have been cheaper, and I would have still had it to this day.

You hear stories of people renovating places only to find that by doing so they have stirred up many spirits. I knew when purchasing this home that it had many different spirits within it. This did not bother me. I was used to beings surrounding me at all times; I figured, what could be different? Well I found out. First of all the walls and floors in this placed had energy imprints of events that had happened in its past. Those things can be removed by many different ways.

The spirits, however, were another matter. Some of them would hang around, though for the most part would not bother me. I would see them at night when I would wake up and see them next to my bed watching me. Or at other times I would be sitting in a chair reading or watching TV and I would look over my shoulder and see them staring at me from the hallway or the kitchen.

There was one ghost that I did not care too much for. It loved to agitate me. On many a occasion I would be walking from the kitchen into the dining room, carrying a plate with the meal I had just prepared. I would suddenly feel a force behind my elbow, pushing violently forward and causing my tray of food to fly across the room and onto the floor. Then I would hear laughing coming from this being. This would happen on multiple occasions and only when I was carrying a glass or a plate of food. My arm would hurt afterwards from each episode. Such spirits feed upon fear so it is important never to give into it. I would just sternly tell it off. Luckily it never happened when company was over.

There was one spirit that I totally did not like. I would have to repeatedly bless the house first with holy water then with holy oils. I would use sage, sweet grass, and cedar to cleanse the rooms. This would calm the ghosts that did stay but I mainly did it to remove one of these spirits that I knew did not like me. This would drive it off, but after a month or two I would start to feel it coming back from a long way. It had a putrid death smell and feel to it. I knew if I did not cleanse and protect the house it would return with vengeance.

One night when it returned I felt its rage that it could not enter. The next morning I had my gutters ripped off the front of the house. Another time it took a part of the siding off my house. The third time I felt it return in a storm. I have felt storms that were natural, and I have also felt when storms contained either energy signatures of a collection of like thoughts we project, or even storms containing spirits within them. On this occasion the spirit had returned.

That was a violent night. The next morning I found that the fencing in the back yard had been torn down and I had parts of another house's roof in my pool. Once I returned from a stay with my parents to find that a one-and-a-half-story tree had been uprooted and come crashing down upon my front door. The seal of protection preventing any damage to the entry way; the tree only damaged the front porch. I had to move twice to finally get rid of one spirit that followed me. But that's another story.

15

My Degrading Health—a Downward Spiral

It's hard to pinpoint a time in my life that I can say was the starting point of my ten years of hell. I would love to say it was this event or that circumstance had caused it. But instead I believe that it was a collection of things that built upon one another until it bubbled forth and changed my life forever. I do think, though, that this time of the constant attacks of these spirits in the house added enough strain to my body to cause it to decline.

I was fighting a battle on many fronts. I did not realize at that time but I was still continuing to develop spiritually. I was not getting any sleep in those years. The vibrational changes on this earth and my declining health all I think contributed to this downward spiral. My mind began to change.

It was subtle at first, but I noticed changes starting to happen. My concentration was no longer as strong as it once had been. I became more and more tired. Time began to warp, or at the very least my perception of it did. Not understanding what was happening, I went to medical doctors for help.

It took years and a lot of self-research to realize how wrong my diagnoses were. If I had only had the answers to my problems ten years ago, I would be one hundred pounds lighter. I would be working through life with no chronic pain and not suffering from the huge debt that I incurred as a direct result of both the medical expenses and costs of living through these times.

I had to address these upsetting changes that were occurring in my thought processes. I found out years later what the true causes were, but at that time I had no clue. After many tests and doctors, I found that there was no physical evidence of any problems that may have caused the mental changes, but they did find what was causing my chest pains upon waking up every morning: I was diagnosed with sleep apnea. I still have not had a good night's sleep since my late twenties. The pain in my other area was another matter. They claimed I had a bad gallbladder. Those doctors convinced me to have it removed.

This was my first of five surgeries in a period of two years. In this procedure I experienced surgical screw-up. They gave me too much anesthesia. I was told later by a nurse that at the time of surgery they miscalculated and put me too far under. This caused my airways to collapse. I came out of this with a tendency to stop breathing whenever I relaxed, plus a viral infection that the doctor denied, claiming it was an unusual case of asthma. I went two months complaining of worse than ever pain in the same region. When I was given antibiotics for an unrelated problem months later, it cleared up the infection I had from this surgery. Prior to the surgery I had a pain in my abdomen. After the surgery I experienced asthma, a throat that collapsed, and a pain in my abdomen.

As for my throat, the problem was that it would collapse upon itself and prevent me from breathing whenever I started to relax. It did not matter if I was standing, sitting, or lying down. The doctors again told me that I had to go under the knife so they could "restructure" the interior of my throat. This took two procedures to prevent my throat from collapsing. I decided I would not go to the same doctor so I went to another surgeon. I did not tell him what had happened, in hopes that they would not talk to each other. When I went under the knife the second time, they did not give me enough anesthetic and I came to in the middle of the surgery. I remembered them cutting me through most of it. The doctor did not believe me weeks later until I told him what he did and what he said through this procedure. I came out of this one with the inability to eat and drink at the same time. It also felt like someone was choking me all the time.

Three surgeries and one year later I came out of this with asthma, pain worse than ever in my abdomen, a throat that felt as though someone were choking me, and my ever changing mind. I started to get worse. I could not keep my eyes open. I would zone out all the time. It was not uncommon for me to start driving somewhere and then come to only to find myself three hours away and across the state. Weeks seem to be hours that had passed, and sometimes hours seem to pass like weeks.

I went to another specialist only to be misdiagnosed with narcolepsy. More medications were prescribed to me. At first it was an interesting feeling. It made my mind operate at an accelerated rate. I could see concepts and ideas I had not grasped before with such clarity and vividness. It gave me energy like I never had before—at least until the tragic day arrived when my body reacted to the medication. I went into a four-day seizure. It wasn't like the typical seizure that an epileptic person would experience. I had to lay on the bed totally motionless. All my thought had to remain blank. Just a minor, quick thought about any part of my body would cause that area and the surrounding areas of my body to violently shake.

This would last as long as my concentration was upon those areas. You don't know how hard it is to lie there day and night trying to blank out a mind. I could not get up, eat, or do much of anything else. For one and a half years, after this event, I thought I was permanently scarred by these drugs. If my body became stressed or tired for any reason, I would go into a seizure.

Sometimes it would only be a part of the body; other times it would be the entire body. I was terrified about telling anyone. I was afraid that people would think less of me. Luckily these episodes became less and less frequent, to the point where they have stopped entirely. The major direct result from these seizures was the way it changed my pathways in my brain. I could no longer reach that duality in the mental process I once had. The ability to have that photographic memory had disappeared also.

I basically had to and still am retraining my brain to re-link a lot of the spiritual pathways I was once able to access and now cannot. My healing ability and connection were lost. I can only tap into a small portion of it as it once was. I felt like a piece of me has died.

Still thinking I had narcolepsy but knowing I did not want to touch any of these drugs, I silently suffered. As the years passed I kept getting worse. It got to a point that I could only remember about ten percent of each day. I took to writing things down and using multiple pads of paper to keep reminding me of things I needed to do and stuff I needed to remember.

In my early thirties I was also diagnosed with diabetes. As I was going through these things a new symptom started to arise and got worse each year. My entire skin felt like it was on fire. When I went out into the sunlight it felt like I had walked into a four-hundred-degree oven. Each year this pain got worse. When I went to multiple doctors to try to get this diagnosed, they would start to look at things but stop as soon as they found out I was a diabetic. They would either tell me it was related to diabetes or neurological symptoms. I kept telling them, "I know what diabetic pain feels like, and I know what this skin pain feels like. And this was not diabetes-related." So I ended up suffering in silence.

In these ten years of hell, I found a few doctors that attempted to help me. They would prescribe to me different types of medications, and the only results from these would be a body that would be taxed under the strain. I would feel weaker and weaker. For every new medication I received, I would gain more weight. Twenty to forty pounds would be added to my body. I would stop the medications, and the weight would stop increasing as well. The weight in turn would cause more inherent problems back upon the body. Each time I stopped going, only to start up again with another doctor when the pain was so unbearable and I could not take it anymore. It was tough dealing with this pain both on the skin and also in the abdomen.

Imagine every place you have skin you have pain. At times when the pain was so unbearable the skin would feel like tissue paper. Your eyelids, the skin in the ear, your armpits, between your toes, and even the skin when you urinate would all feel it. The only relief I would get would be to stand in front of a fan and let it blow on my skin. It would change the feeling from pain to another sensation that was more tolerable. Clothing would be an issue. Even simple things like deodorant would cause an increase in the pain.

At first I would take the exercises I had originally developed in order to attempt to split my consciousness into two halves. I would use a part of my mind to consciously take the pain sensation in both the abdomen and skin and block the feeling entirely. When I could no longer do that then I used that portion of the brain to change the feeling of the pain to another sensation. This would work for most of the time, but after a while a portion of my brain would start to ache and tire. Combining that with the ever-increasing memory loss, this process became less and less effective. Yes I could block the pain from my consciousness, but my body still felt it. I started to see the direct results of what this pain was doing to my body and literally my mind.

What could I do? I repeatedly asked for help from my angels. I yelled to God for help. I saw any doctor I could with no result. My mind was failing me, and I became the sole witness to it. I was losing my memories from childhood, my twenties, and now even events that transpired from day to day. I could no longer concentrate. It was getting harder and harder for me to apply only the simple techniques to stop some of the pain. I spent weekends and nights crying, wanting my pain to stop. I asked for help from everyone and everything I knew, but I felt I was abandoned. I was alone and helpless.

16

At My Lowest Point, with Nowhere to Turn

People for the most part do not understand why one would consider ending one's life. In my younger days I never really put much thought into it. I did not believe taking one's life caused one to go to hell. I would have to believe in a hell in the first place to even consider that one.

I do believe a soul that is tormented carries these events as they transfer from this life to the next. I knew and have heard of people who had taken their life for one reason or another. I did not truly appreciate why one would do so until my late thirties. I tried everything I could to find even a moment in time where I could feel at peace. I knew what it felt like on the other side, and I knew what I was feeling in my body. I felt alone, isolated and rejected. My mind was gone. I could no longer remember my past or even day-to-day events.

I kept forgetting little things like paying bills. Had I taken my medication, and if so which ones? I was having trouble at work. I could no longer remember the steps to do tasks that I had originally designed and set up at the company I worked for. I would not know if I would be wake up at home or somewhere else. The constant pain both in my abdomen and my skin kept a constant vigil.

I can remember waking up one night suddenly. As I came to, I felt peace in my body. I can remember clearly what it felt like lying there, joyous at experiencing what I had not felt in years. Then it hit me, the sudden wave of pain. It felt ten times more intense, hitting me like a brick alongside the head. Abandoned by both this world and the next, I wanted to return home to the other side. It was little bits of time at first, a thought here and a thought there.

I was broken and tired and could not take life anymore. Yes I did think of dying. The more the pain became the more I entertained the thought. Looking back on these years, there were three times in my life that I resolved myself to end it. I can remember sitting in the chair or on the couch saying to myself, *I cannot take it anymore.* I wanted the pain to end. I was mad at God and my angels. I stopped talking to them for over a year because of the anger I felt toward them. I had given my entire life to the pursuit of God and my role in his Divine plan. I passed up on relationships, wealth, and happiness so I could attempt to understand how I fit into it. After the loss of my connection to the other side, from the seizure, I literally felt everyone and everything had left me.

On all three occasions I sat staring off into space, thinking that I had made the decision to die, to end my life. And what transpired each time was the same. I will tell you what happened the first time. My mind, body, and spirit came to the conclusion that this was it. I would force the interaction of God with me by returning home. And so I decided to end it. There comes a moment in time when every part of yourself decides on the correct course of action. A realization comes over you. You become at peace. You no longer fear. I had this anticipation of finally returning home. With a joyous feeling, my body rang out. My mind yearned for the return. It was not the welcome home I would have liked, but to return would have been good enough. At this moment when all parts of yourself arrive at this point, you change. I felt acceptance.

Then it happened. I saw it both in my mind's eye and in the flesh. Two large angels, each one grabbing one of my shoulders and armpits, lifted me up. The room filled with love. I felt like I was floating on air. In my mind's eye I saw and felt as if I was a baby wrapped upon in a mother's arms. At first I struggled with them, wanting to end my life. They would have none of that. The more I struggled to return home, the more they held me with their healing love radiating out of them. I would feel them holding me for days at a time, until the feeling of wanting to return home ended. Then they would disappear. I wished they would tell me what I had to do to stop the pain. They would never speak any words, but they always kept a constant presence next to me.

To this day I've never understood why I've been treated so differently from the people I knew around me. I had seen the interaction of spirit with my friends. Some would get voices communicating. Others would get flashes of images before their eyes, and still some would get comfort in dreams. I never have gotten any of those things.

I wish I could say it was that experience that transformed my life, and in some way it did. This and other experiences did not transform me consciously or remove my pain. They never gave me the insights as to why it was happening. What they would do is at my lowest times I have been in, they would step in and allow me the grace to feel the Divine love. Then they would leave when my lowest points had passed. I loved and hated them for it. Abandoned by modern medicine and not receiving any answers from spirit, I was angry, mad at everyone. I still find myself at times frustrated at not understanding why they would not allow my body to heal or to find a medical doctor to treat my symptoms. And I suffer every day in my silence for it.

17

The Long Road Back

This journey back has been a long one. I never have been able to remove the pain, and I deal with it every day. I've come to accept the fact that I will never have the ability to control my mind in the same ways I did in my earlier years. Even though I still practice healing through the laying of hands, I also know I will never be able to reach to the extent in the abilities I once had. My memories of my childhood, my teen years, my twenties, and even in my thirties are lost in the recesses of my mind, with a few exceptions of pieces here and there.

It's a strange feeling, being forced to live in the moment, not being able to remember or to relive the memories of my past. With the pain and events that transpire in the present, I find myself not wanting to look toward the future. I now deal in the present.

At times I wonder if that was one of the reasons spirit added these obstacles in my path: to force me to live in the day, to taking each moment and treasuring it as long as I can knowing that I might not be able to remember pieces of it in days, months, or years to come. It's not that I'm no longer learning new things.

That is not true; I am relearning things and bringing forth them into my consciousness in a different form. I had to rethink my outlook so as to experience life in a new way, as if I had been reborn anew.

I still rush to the emergency room a couple of times a year when the pain changes suddenly or if I cannot take it anymore, only to find to my relief that nothing has ruptured or needs surgery. I have been able to recapture my attention and focus to some degree. I know with great amount of concentration I can train all my thoughts to one beam of intent.

I can no longer keep up that concentration up for hours. It only lasts a few minutes, but it is an improvement. I can still occasionally tap into the tonal vibrations of other realms and draw upon the energies of angels and high level beings, but I now have to be really careful. My body can no longer tolerate the intense vibrations for any periods of time. The pain in my skin keeps increasing till it feels like I've stepped into a four-hundred-degree oven. My ulcers start to increase in pain, and my digestive system starts to hurt.

I do miss dealing with those energies. If I were asked if I'd known what would happen in my later life if I started doing what I did in my twenties, would I still do it, my answer would be YES. I did not have a choice in this situation. Being dragged along my life by spirit and my higher self, I still would have chosen to have that rope tied around me, though I would try to avoid some of the larger rocks I tripped over and smashed against along the way.

I do feel bad that through these painful years of my life I became short with people. The closer I was to someone the shorter my speech was. I was constantly aware that I had to keep my emotions in check. I knew that we human beings, as Divine as our souls are, have the capability to use both positive and negative energies. I knew I was capable of using Divine light extremely well, but I also had knowledge that I could use that negative energy with the same power.

Only in moments when everything became too intense for me to handle would I vent some of that anger toward someone. I realized in a only few short seconds the damage I had done with what I said or how I looked at someone. I would see and feel this blackness and intense, dark energy shoot out of myself with such force and lower energy that I had to quickly recapture it and dissipate it with the Divine light energy.

I am truly sorry for the reactions I have gotten from my targeted rage. I did not physically strike anyone, but the intense energy had a more damaging intent. How could I tell my family, friends, and coworkers that I was doing everything in my power to keep this side of me under wraps? I could not tell any one of them that the fuel for this rage was the constant pain.

After the seizure I felt disconnected from my spiritual side. The memory loss kept getting worse, and I could only remember ten percent of each day and in a few days I would lose most of that. I could not explain to them that I felt kicked out of both the spirit world as well as this physical one. How could I explain to them that the debt I had incurred which kept me on the brink of bankruptcy?

I was dealing on a daily bases with the constant medical excursions and prescriptions and with intense mood swings from anger to depression and back again. All these issues piled on top of each other, compressing and building pressure that tried to find ways to burst its confinement.

I was afraid that if I let just a minute amount out, I would not be able to control what might happen. I was afraid of that. I told myself that the minor, sharp, intense energy outbreaks were small in comparison to allowing the build-up of the anger, frustration, and confusion I might otherwise release upon this world.

It is not like nothing had happened spiritually after my downfall. I still had events in my life that allowed me glimpses into the spirit realm. For the most part they were not as intense or as frequent as they once were. It took a lot of years to overcome my limitations and finally accept that I could no longer be what I once was and that was ok. I knew somewhere in myself I had the ability to start again, to figure out what my new talents were. I picked up the pieces, tossed what I no longer could use, and started out again. I do have relapses from time to time.

I keep reminding myself through these episodes that there will be better times ahead. I take the pain in stride each day. I accept this burden on my shoulders, waiting for the time I can unload it for the last time. I have always had an issue with how things happened in my life. I always told my guides and angels as well as God that I would go through anything that was asked of me. I only wanted to be kept in the loop. This is something they never did. It was years later in my life before I could truly understand only a portion of what I had to go through and why.

18

Brain Surgery

I have always had many different types of dreams. I find that the most common type of dreams consists of random patterns of images, sounds, and feelings grouped together to form a non-coherent movie. A lot of these I feel come from your subconscious mind trying to sort out the events that have recently happened.

By sorting these random events your mind comes to a conclusion about what has been on your conscious mind. This group of dreams is not what I want to discuss now. The next forms of dreams come from the mind-states where you're half in and half out of this reality. You see spirits or hear them. This type of dream is like a more fluid movie. What it teaches are coherent patterns of thought that form an idea.

I truly feel that it is communication either with your higher self or with your guides and angels. A third type of dream are ones formed by astral traveling either to locations on this side or in other realms. This particular dream state is what I would like to discuss now.

I have a set of dreams that I like to call lifetimes on the other side. These have spanned across my entire life and are one continuous movie. When I'm in this altered state, I remember other visitations in my past. The people and places build upon each other, layered one upon on another as if I'm experiencing a life I'm living parallel to the one I'm living now.

When I'm in this altered life I can draw upon previous experiences I have had in those places. In each reality I visit, those people that are tied to each world reappears time and time again. As I'm experiencing these dreams I feel I have free will control to change anything in them as I can in this reality. The dreams all have a unique feel to them. They are totally different than other states of visitations to the other side, visits from my guides, and just standard dreams. They are as real as I am sitting here writing this.

In one particular visit I can remember coming to in an abandoned warehouse in a particular section of town. This place was off a dirt road located slightly upon a hill. I can remember looking back in the middle of the street down toward the road that intersected the main stretch of a thoroughfare running perpendicular to it. The structures in the town are between three and five stories high.

Each building along this stretch of roadway was similar in nature as they all had red brick exteriors and white cement trim. It looked like this area had been abandoned for a long time. Rusted objects lay everywhere. Some rusted metal tanks were suspended on platforms located along the back of one building to the left side of the street. This place looked like it had been deserted for a long time. I knew that there were farmhouses and fields within miles of this place.

From the nature of this layout I figured it couldn't be a typical industrial complex. I stood at the highest point on the street and looked around. You could see down the hill and across the road. As far as my eyes could see, there were miles of farming fields. Some had cows in them and others did not. Some looked like they were once used to grow food but had not had a crop in recent years.

I started to walk up the street to have a look. I felt the gravel under my feet. This did not feel like a dream. I got near the end of the road I was on, and I knew after two more buildings farther that the main street curved to the right. Something in the fourth floor window in the second to the last building on the right caught my eye. This building was the tallest one there. It had a total of five floors. I noticed that the door to the front of the building was open. It was a wider door than normal. I decided to go in and investigate.

Inside, this building had what looked like a main hallway that stretched from the entrance to the back. Doors were located on each side of this walkway. Everything in this building had large doors, large hallways, and large rooms. It reminded me of a combination hospital and research lab. The interior looked like the size of a small warehouse. I thought to myself that appearances were deceiving.

What it looked like on the outside did not match what was actually inside the building. A wide, iron stairway was located off to the side toward the back of this main walkway. I walked up the stairs. I headed straight to the fourth floor. I wanted to find out what I had seen flicker in that window. I went to the room that I thought I saw movement in and entered.

This room, unlike the others, had cabinets along the wall. It looked like a medical room with a combination table–chair apparatus in the middle. It had a hole through the top end of it. There were round, circular lights hanging from the ceiling. I thought to myself that this was too surreal. I looked around the room. Then I approached the window and looked out. From this view I could see the layout of the row of buildings along the street. I knew then that this was not a city but only a few buildings alongside one another.

I turned around then. I told myself that I needed to leave and in a hurry. The panic welled up in me. I knew I had been here before but could not remember it. I did not want to remember. It was a nightmare I never wanted to bring into focus again. I did not like this. So I started to head toward the door.

When I got about ten feet from the door a group of people stepped out of the shadows. Some were dressed in suits, and some had white lab coats on. They told me not to be alarmed. They had brought me here for a reason and I was to sit on the metal chair-like table in the middle of the room. All my will and desire left. I felt I could not move anywhere but only toward that strange looking metal table.

I sat down facing the open end of the hole. They then told me to lean forward and put my face through the opening. I felt the straps being applied and tightened, locking my head down in place. I could not move. I tried to, but the restrains held me tight. I was also told then that ten years ago they had made some changes to my brain and messed up on some of the rewiring.

To correct the worst damage they needed to go back into my skull to repair some of the mishaps. What could I do? I did not want any of this to happen. I was terrified, but I had no choice in the matter.

Then a strange thing happened. I felt no pain, but I did feel what they did to me and where they did it. I felt them cut the base of my skull off and expose my brain. I felt the breeze lightly hit the exposed surface of my brain. I started to panic. They calmed me down and said it would be a few more minutes. Then I felt these probes enter through my brain in three locations, heading toward the center. The first rod went into the middle back section. The second then headed from the top of my exposed brain. Finally the third rod came in from the right side. These rods were hollow. I felt them insert other instruments into them. They sounded like high-speed drills. I could feel them penetrate deeper into parts of my brain.

I had flashes of matter splattering everywhere. I did feel them move things around in there. I began to panic and tried with all my might to get free from the restraints. A female nurse—I could only see her hands and part of her front lab coat—approached the front of me. She held out her hands and placed them firmly on both sides of my temples.

She told me to remain calm and said it would be over soon. It was then when I faded to sleep. I woke up the next morning with my brain feeling unusually weird. I ran to the bathroom looking for any scars or damage. I could not find any noticeable damage. I did not expect too, either.

I have never told anyone of this experience. I didn't want wanting to mention what I was going through with both the trips and my mental changes. I kept it all to myself, feeling ashamed of what was happening. I felt I was violated, and I could not lash out. Who could I turn to? As for going to the police, though it would have been a funny sight to see, I would have never considered doing such a thing. However, years later I was sitting with a good friend of mine at a restaurant.

She had gone into a deep channel and relayed to me a message about this incident. The messages went into detail about these events and explained why it had to be done. I had never told her or anyone of what had happened. Her relaying in detail of what had happened had made me believe her even more. At the time this had happened, I wondered if this was an E.T. experience. It was too real to be a dream, and I never watch horror movies. I did not have a clue. What I did know was that this was a real place I had seen. I knew this had happened, even if it went against what society considered normal.

19

The Reason for the Rewire

We go through life trying to lead a normal and happy existence. We rely heavily with our five senses when trying to piece together parts of awareness that can be seen, heard, felt, and experienced. When you encounter pieces of yourself that are awakened and are not of the five senses, you see patterns and shapes that run against what your conscious mind is telling you.

We have many filters in place to sift through these levels of awareness created by these new abilities. You know you experience these events but in the translation to our limited brain you wonder how much has gotten distorted and misfiled. It is easy to relay a story of an event that transpired in one day of your life, but to try to put events that transcend this reality into pictures and words becomes tricky.

There are many times in our lives that we revisit an experience and, with the additional events we've subsequently lived through, the spiritual significance of the event changes. It is not that our original understanding of the event was wrong, but our interpretation of it becomes different. I have always told spirit

83

that if they would just keep me in the loop of these spiritual episodes, I would not have to spend so much time sorting out a meaning from them.

What I knew up to this point is that my brain, over the course of eight years, had changed. Many times it happened so suddenly I thought I was losing my mind. I knew I did not have the gifts I once had. I knew the trips to the other side had reduced dramatically. I understood that time itself seem to change. It would warping and combine, and as a result large parts of my day would disappear. I would be at work concentrating upon something, and the next thing I knew it would be hours later and I had not moved. I no longer remembered my past.

The memories of my childhood, teen years, and adult life disappeared. I accepted all this, figuring it was a drug-induced seizure that had changed all this. Was it really this, or had it been something else? Yes, I could chalk it up in part to the seizure, but it did not explain the whole picture. There were two many things that were left out. There were pieces of this puzzle that had disappeared, and I could no longer find them.

All my life I have been able to know what kind of spirit that would suddenly appear around me. One class of spirits were multiple-dimensional beings, the dons of the universe is what I call them. I don't know much about them but do feel them come and go in my life. I know that I am under a microscope, being observed by these spirits.

For some reason they have taken an interest in my life, along with the recent changes on planet earth. These beings are so far distant that they do not interact with this reality much. When they do take an active role, many spirits and angels help them. This I think is to insure that the energies become compatible. They do not speak to me as my guides do, but when they do come around I do feel them. Their tonal energies are so unique they do take some time to get used to.

I can remember one fall day a friend and I decided to spend a few hours one Sunday afternoon catching up on things that had happened in our normal lives. She is a medium herself. I had never explained to her what had happened to me with my brain being changed. This I'd kept to myself. As I was sitting in this new restaurant enjoying her company, she went into a semi-trance.

She proceeded to explain to me that she was being pulled far out from this reality into an area she had never been to before. Then she was taken to a circle with these beings. As those high-level, multi-dimensional beings began speaking she started to tell me the reasons why I was going through these changes in my brain. She told me that I was the one of the prototypes for the re-wiring of the brain. My higher self had decided to allow these beings to experiment on me.

My so-called sacrifice was happening in order to allow others on this planet to go through an easier time than I'd had. She then said that these changes were needed for a couple of reasons. First was the changes in the earth and the vibration changes human kind will be going through.

Second, our consciousness had been changed to allow the melting of the left and right sides of the brain to allow new spiritual development for generations to come. As she came out of it, she told me she never in her life had gone so far out and she'd never stretched her capabilities to the point where she could perceive these types of beings.

She never knew they existed up to this point. I then proceeded to let her know who they were and my understanding of what they are. It has been interesting since then because she can now tune into their energies and on occasion see them around me. It is a nice confirmation because where she will point them out, I know they are there because I do feel their presence.

Does this give me peace in understanding that the hell I went through was caused by them and not by myself? To some degree it does. Even though on some level I have agreed to this arrangement between them and myself, it is still sometimes uncomfortable. I am fascinated and nervous with them. However, they are in some degree a part of me now.

About six months later someone had told me about a web site with a person who had been channeling spirits for years now and I should check him out. When reviewing the videos I was hit like a ton of bricks. I had always felt alone on this journey, thinking I was the only one feeling and experiencing these unusual events.

This man channeled in spirit and talked about everything I had experienced and lived through. At times I had actually thought he had somehow read my mind. He also had explained about this rewiring. That is when all the pieces fell into place. I'm not crazy. This is real. I did experience these things. Someone on the other side of the United States, a total stranger, was speaking of the events that I had lived through.

20

The Cry for Help

In dealing with the order of the universe, we naturally gravitate to like vibrations. What we perceive and how we feel generally attracts like vibrations to it. Of course there are loopholes in this type of thinking. In cases where, prior to coming into this life we have agreed to experience an event in order to learn from it, then those energies will gravitate toward you. To the degree of the cause and effect is largely dependent upon the changes you make while down upon this learning school of life. There are other situations where your mind and soul, in desperation, reach out to energies and vibrations that will help then break free from the confinements that they themselves have formed.

I have never paid much attention to spirits in need or low-vibration energy spirits. It was not my lot in life to give them anything other than a passing thought. When I would encounter one, I would recognize it then move on. The apartment complexes where I live has people moving in and out all the time.

When an apartment is empty it generally fills back up with another group within a month of the old renters moving out. I have seen my next-door neighbor change many times over the years, until the eventful day when the last group of people had moved out and something else moved in. This place remained unoccupied for four months, not the usual three weeks. I knew why. I could not tell you where this man in spirit came from or how he had noticed me.

I felt this spirit's fear of me right from the start. I also noticed that he was at the same time drawn to my energies. I was aware of him right away. As I would come up the walk to my door I would see him about four to six feet back from the window standing either in the kitchen or the living room looking back at me. His anger I felt within twenty-five feet from my door. I spent weeks feeling uncomfortable with his angry stare. I acted like I didn't notice him and as quickly as I could I would open and close my door.

I have had friends walk into and out of my apartment saying that they loved the energy and feeling inside but hated the walkway and the front door. The way the apartments were laid out both doors faced each other and both windows that looked into the kitchen and living room faced perpendicular in relation to the walkway heading up to both doors.

After dealing with the intrusion on my life for weeks, I asked my angels why was he here. They responded that he was a confused and an angry spirit, but his higher self, disconnected as it was to his conscious self, was trying to stretch out and find help. He needed desperately to get himself out of his low-level vibration.

He was seeking for the Divine light, and though he yearned for it he did not know how to find it. They then told me that there was something in my divine light that he recognized and at the same time was terrified of. His conscious self knew that I had a piece of his puzzle, part of the answers he sought. I told my guides that I did not want him in the house, though I knew I did not need to say it, since I have always felt the Divine protection on the walls of this place. It is a sanctuary for me; I consider this a place of refuge.

Days later I received another message from my spirits that what also attracted him to me was that he noticed all the higher-vibration angels coming to and going from my place. When I went somewhere I would feel his presence walking behind me or off to my side about fifteen feet back, daring not to approach closer. I could feel his yearning to come close, but I also knew he dared not out of fear. At times I could feel his anger, confusion, and low-level vibration quite strongly.

On one night I was walking a friend of mine to her car when she commented that the walkway had never felt this bad in days past. I then told her to look into the vacant apartment window and tell me what she could see. She peered in. It only took about three seconds for her to move backward, being a little startled. She then proceeded to tell me of a man in spirit and what he looked like. It was the same one I had seen.

She then stepped back to the window and looked in again. She then told me that this spirit became even angrier for the attention she was giving it. I felt at that moment he was ashamed. That night changed everything. For a week afterward, even though I had seen him in the apartment I could not stop thinking about this man, and I could not remove his energy from my thoughts. It became very uncomfortable at times. When I could no longer bear it anymore, I asked my angels why. The only thing I got from them is *Let him in*. I said NO! They then repeated those same words, *Let him in*.

After a day of arguing with my guides, and knowing that he was not leaving, I sat down and told my guides I would do it on my terms. First of all this spirit would be accompanied by my guides at all times. He was not allowed to remain in my place when I slept, nor to affect, move, or make disappear anything in the apartment. Then it happened. I felt him approach closer. His energy felt overwhelming, a bit terrifying. At the same time

I also felt my angels closer and stronger than ever. Looking back on it, it was an interesting feeling, both high and low vibration levels at the same time.

I felt this spirit with me both day and night, when I went to work and when I came home. I kept telling him to go to the light. I must admit, my tone wasn't peaceful and full of Divine grace as it should have been. It was blunt and forceful. I must have repeated those words twenty times a day for days on end. Then as quickly as he came, he left. At times I stretch out my vibrational energy and touch him. His energy has improved, and he has moved on. I ended up doing a wonderful thing in the grand scheme of things, but I went kicking and screaming all the way. That same apartment became rented with new tenants within days of him leaving.

21

You Saw What?

In the many years I have spent striving for the Divine God within, I have put a lot of thought and energy into feeling the presence of God and how his vibration interacts with other vibrations. I have never set out as a goal to feel energy shifts and tonal vibration waves. This was an unexpected and pleasant side effect. At times I have regrets, but overall I would not trade it for anything.

I have seen and heard spirits with lower energy vibrations. It is not something that happens constantly. If you would have told me that the years I spent in finding God and my role in his grand design of things would cause me to sense multi-level beings, spirits, guides, thoughts of other people, and changes around me, I would have told you were crazy. One does not go out of their way to pursue this type of medium ship.

One particular episode started out like any other day, with me traveling in the afternoon to a local grocery store. As I was coming up upon the entrance to the side road that led me to this place, I noticed about thirty feet from me a lady making a right turn. That's all it took. I felt my consciousness pull out from my physical body.

I saw this in my mind's eye. My thought processes altered. I felt myself split into many different trains of thought. It was as if I became a set of multiple me's existing slightly out of phase with each other. I had each individual thought running simultaneously. No one mind-thought was stronger than any of the others. One of my consciousnesses stretched out and literally zoomed up onto the face of the driver.

The second consciousness stretched out to a twelve-year-old kid on a bike pedaling fast down the sidewalk. I saw both of them at the same time transposed upon each other. Their thoughts separated but at the same time came forth in my mind. The lady at the wheel was getting tired of waiting to pull out in traffic to hang a right. She then said she would step on it when an opening came.

The kid's consciousness was different. I felt him as a part of him was leaving his body. I then knew he did not see the silver car in front of him ten feet away. The lady's consciousness relayed to me that she did not see the kid on his bike.

She stepped on the accelerator. The kid on the bike was in front of the car at the time. His bike flipped sideways, and both he and the bike went under the car. Another consciousness zoomed out and showed in detail the front end of the car. With the recent acceleration, the front end of the vehicle lifted up. Her mind told me that she panicked.

As my consciousness could not expand anymore an image arose in my mind's eye of a monster's mouth clamping down on its prey. Each time it tried to get a bigger piece, only at the last minute its prey would slip away. My mind stretched again. In my sight, bubbles appeared from the enlarged image on the front end of the car. One bubble on his right leg, one on his left leg, and the third on his torso, back and face.

At this time the overall scene could be compared to when, in a karate movie, an actor is gliding along kicking his feet backwards against his opponent. To say the least, it was surreal. I noticed that his jacket and back clothing became distorted. Strange, I thought.

Then my mind expanded again. Silhouettes of multiple angels formed. One pulled on his left leg, one on his right, and the rest wrapped around his torso pulling to free him from this imposed beast. Then when I thought it could not stretch any more, my consciousness expanded even further. I zoomed up toward the bike and his legs. The car clamped down on the kid and his bike. I watched the tires and frame of the bike bend in half. When his feet were milliseconds away from being ensnared into the tangle, and angel would pull his feet away.

It seemed to happen over and over again. The kid was in front of the car, sideways, being flown backwards by the force of the car's momentum and finally stopping ten feet into the roadway. Every piece of split consciousness that had been created from me then snapped back into my body with force. The first thing I noticed was how exhausted I became in those few short seconds.

Secondly I noticed that when the kid jumped up to confront the woman behind the wheel, he had suddenly aged. He did not look like the twelve-year-old kid I had seen only moments before. He appeared to be a seventeen-year-old. He had grown taller. His posture was different. I look down and realized I had stopped in the middle of the road, had my seat belt off, and was already climbing out of the door. Then I realized that I had stopped traffic behind me before the incident. It was only hours after I became aware that if I had not stopped moments before, the vehicle behind me would have hit the kid.

What had happened? I could not explain. All I know is that it did happen. I was physically, mentally, and emotionally drained from this experience. Strangely it wasn't from seeing this poor child go through this tragic ordeal, but it came from what I experienced on another level.

I went days after with many ranges of emotions, even feelings I had never felt before. I flopped back and forth between guilt, worry, anxiousness, and an influx of vibrations. I cycled through them, each emotion bubbling fourth to the surface, desiring to express themselves only to disappear and another one take its place. Was this the byproduct of the spiritual experience I had experienced?

It took days to finally have these feelings die down enough to function normally. I strangely felt as though I had said or done something that upset a lot of people. It was like I'd been on a date that went wrong. I knew this was not the case, but it did not relieve the feelings that went through me.

22

The Divine Energy Pathways

By now you must think that my life was an easy one. The spiritual events and knowledge must have come to me quickly and with little or no effort. Of course not only is this untrue, but in fact it had been complete the opposite. When most people spent their energies on a life with a spouse, kids, and a mortgage payment, I spent my time focusing my thoughts and energies on abstract concepts.

I tested and then re-tested these ideas over and over again until I found the right combination to prove or disprove these theories. All I had to lean on was the compelling drive to pursue certain areas and ideas and the internal awareness of whether I was on the right track or not. I may have gotten the names and descriptions wrong in some cases, but the energies I feel have been correct and true. In this particular case it was no different.

My awareness of a multi-dimensional universe came to me long after my downfall from the seizure and the re-wiring of my brain. I had to find other ways to tap into this universe, and I knew that the way I had previously done it was no longer obtainable. I knew up to this point that every time I would find a breakthrough in healing with the Divine, spirit would reset my thought processes and I would have to start on another route. When I would break through the veil and tap into the Divine energy using a particular technique, I would get amazing results, but then things would change.

One particular time I was trying to find another route to the Divine by tracing energy pathways. An imprint began to form. I will try to describe it the best way I can. Imagine slicing an onion in half; with closer inspection you will notice each layer is separated by a thin membrane. It's like an LP record, with blank spaces between each song.

Each layer is a reality. Groups of like vibrating energies by their very nature gravitate toward the layer that they are harmonizing best at. At the core of this onion is, for a lack of better image, a blazing sun. This is the Divine God, God creator, and Heavenly Father, whatever name you want to call it. This Divine energy contains an infinite number of roots that branch from its surface and head throughout all the layers. Each branch of roots leads into the Divine energy of everything. A branch starts from the surface of God and ends at the spark of the Divine within each of us. These branches not only end in each human being but also in every divine spark. Every energy signature that gives of its own tonal vibration has its own connection to the Divine God.

Some branch root systems are thick, and some are thin, but all are connected. If we slice off section of a root, we will notice the manna, the true Divine energy that is passed freely from God to us and then back again. I have noticed that by traveling upon this highway of energy you can increase its flow, making your connection root system stronger and larger. Our individual bodies themselves cannot make the complete trip from your tip of the root to the surface of the Divine God, but by aligning your other pieces of yourself you can jump from one level to another and another till you eventually hit the surface of the Divine God. This can only be obtained by using your Divine self.

I have also noticed that not only can you follow the main pathway from you to the Divine, you can also use this same energy highway from you to another soul. You can travel through it to a plant or an animal. Anything that is connected to it by the root system can be tapped into. Though this small change in intent you can bypass any walls and blocks that someone may have up. Of course by just being in the flow of this lifeblood, you naturally obey the universal laws and cannot do any harm to another.

Let's go back to the membrane between the layers of reality. This membrane serves multiple purposes. It allows each reality to stretch and shrink by the direct results of the influx of Divine blood flowing through each vein while preventing two realities from collapsing into each other. The other purpose of this is to protect the integrity of the root system itself. Look at a shift in tectonic plates. When two realities shift, it causes the contact points to buckle and shatter. This membrane allows the flow of Divine blood between each reality. When the events of both realities, layers, start to change dramatically, there will not be any broken connections from the root system itself.

When focusing my energy on this membrane I stumbled upon these energy beings that reside within each membrane. For a lack of a better name I will refer to them as energy beings. They do not contain any humanistic tonal vibrations. They have never lived a life upon this or any other planet or layer of reality. The by-product of the Divine energy flowing through the root system transferring from one reality to the next created them.

These beings have a very unique energy signature. They want to help. They themselves maintain the integrity of each root system. They gain their knowledge and understanding from it. With permission from the angels and guides of each reality layer they are allowed from time to time to come into a layer and help. In the next chapter I will explain in detail my experience with these wonderful beings.

Each layer is a reality. We are in the middle of this onion. Our reality is one of the most unique ones within this onion. It is the physical realm. It is the only one, that I'm aware of, that allows both the physical manifestation and the energy imprints. It allows each one of us, once we recognize our own Divine God within, to mold the energies into a physical form. We all do it on some level. In the first stages we manifest the physical forms of our ideas through physical efforts. As we begin to grow and learn how to mold the Divine energies, we will be able to mold physical forms by the grouping of vibrations and energies.

23

The Beings Between the Realms and Realities

I have, on occasion, done the laying of hands in a couple of churches I attend. Even though I got good comments from the people I have worked on, I was never totally satisfied with the results. I was always comparing it to what I was able to do in my twenties.

On one particular occasion my angels told me that those new energy beings I'd discovered wanted to help me in my healing abilities. I accepted their help. I felt my angels allowing them to come forth whenever I was working on someone. My skin pain would start to flair up. My arms would begin to feel like they were on fire. My back felt like someone had dumped gasoline on it, then threw a lit match on it, igniting my back in a heated blaze.

These energy beings had great power. They could raise the temperature in the room considerably. In a matter of minutes they could increase the heat in the room by ten degrees.

In the days and months I worked with them I silently laughed, because during those times I did healing not only would I be drenched in sweat with my shirt soaked through, the people next to me healing were also going through some of the intense heat as well. After each session they would comment on how hot it had gotten in the room and how much energy they had felt.

I never have told them that it was largely due to these energy beings that I was working with. I wanted to see how far I could go with them. I knew their energy patterns were not exactly compatible with the energies on this realm. I asked my angels about this. They explained to me that I needed to convert this energy signature into a more compatible format. I needed to learn to transform this into a source of raw Divine energy that can be used into this realm. This fascinated me. They also told me it was an experiment that had never been accomplished before. It was needed to see what could and could not be used.

Off I went, drawing more and more energy into myself, mixing it with my energies, and sending it out again. It was like a drug-induced high. I wanted to see how far I could take it, and I also wanted to see the effects it was having on not only the other healers but also the people I laid my hands on. Just when I thought I could no longer draw any more raw energy, I stretched my mind and focused to absorb a tiny bit more. Even though this energy was not the same as what I used earlier in life, for the first time since the seizures and rewiring I was able to develop to a level of healing I was close to what was accustomed to--that is until the uneventful day when things came crashing down.

I was donating my time in a healing service, drawing upon greater and greater reserves of this energy to change, mold, and manifest into this reality. The temperature increased in this room dramatically. I noticed the person that was healing next to me was drenched in sweat. I tried like many times before to increase this flow.

Then it happened. I saw it both as if it had happened physically and also in my mind's eye. It started from my left shoulder and then continued to rapidly tear down to my lower right hip. My skin, organs, and muscles felt like they were shredding apart, splitting open as if someone had sliced me with a sword. The pain was intense. I knew what had happened. I had split my energetic self and created a huge, gaping hole. Suddenly I felt the energy beings quickly backing away. My guides surrounded me. I heard them say that the experiment was over, that I had taken in more than I should have and the incompatibilities were too great.

This had cause a great rip within my spiritual self. They said that I would be protected and that no harm would come to me while this was being repaired. They also told me that I would no longer be using these beings in the same way again. They then told me that my healing abilities would be greatly eliminated until I could be fixed and balanced. I was physically, mentally, and spiritually exhausted. I felt totally drained. They were right: I could not draw upon any healing for six months, at which point they felt I was ready to continue. Ironically, I had to re-learn again another path to healing.

24

They Do Exist!

I have to admit it. I have no problems talking to anyone about my accomplishments with my healing. I can discuss the visits from dimensional beings and even tell my tales about my trips to other realities. However, I sit here now finding it hard to write about an event that happened in my life in the not-too-distant past. I vacillated for days wondering if I should include it or not in this book. You can already tell what side had won. I reached a decision to relay my story as accurately as I can remember and allow you to be the judge whether this is real or not. As for myself, I believe it happened.

This story starts, as most of mine do in recent years, with my health. The current medication I was taking for the skin pain had started to begin to have a less of an effect, so the doctor prescribed a stronger variation of this medication. Even though it was effective in reducing this pain considerably and the side-effects of fatigue were tolerable, in a few short days the pain in my ulcers started becoming intense. I stopped this new drug. The pain continued to be in the forefront. After a week went by some stability started to appear in this discomfort. So when a friend of mine mentioned that her mother was giving a talk at a light center an hour north of me I decided to go.

The lady that runs this place is a medium who channels Archangel Raphael. Always interested in meeting unique people I was excited to head up there and see her in person. The only thing holding me back was my discomfort. Feeling the best I had felt in a couple of days, I decided to see what all the interest was about. When I entered this place, the energy hit me like a ton of bricks.

Each spirit, angel, guide, and being gives off unique tonal vibrations. Archangels are no different. They have, to me, a light, refined, peaceful feeling—a very loving vibration and yet quite different than what you or I have. It usually makes me feel like I'm floating on air. This place was full of it. Every time I experience the energy of an archangel, a part of me changes. I always leave it feeling changed forever. I thought to myself that the reason I was there was to have the energies heal my pain, but I found out that wasn't the case.

Soaking up the energy in the room, I sat quietly off to the side. I didn't pay much attention to my surroundings but instead focused on feeling the love of Archangel Raphael. The lecture then began. My mother's friend, who I might add is a beautiful soul in her own right, started to speak. She is an alien abductee and has written a couple of books on the subject.

As if on cue I felt the loving archangel's presence begin to recede. In my mind's eye I saw clouds of a very different energy began to hover over the house. I glanced outside from the window next to me and noticed the sun had disappeared and a gray sky had emerged. Both feeling the changes happening and physically seeing them happen had suddenly wakened me out of my hazy daze. I became very alert and noticed many changes starting to unfold on many levels. I no longer felt the presence of Archangel Raphael. I was told in my mind that he receded to allow a different type of presence to appear.

Focusing on the new energy, which was of a type I hadn't encountered before, I started to feel slightly off-phase. I did not like what I was experiencing. My stomach pain did not like it either. I pushed ahead, allowing this energy to flow through my conscious mind. It got more intense. Then it happened. First a cloud of dull gray matter appeared about four feet from the ground. It had a foggy, translucent appearance. I went deeper. First I saw shadows within this fog. Then the shadows became more apparent. They had the same translucent appearance but were very distinguishable from each other. I told my higher self I needed to become invisible to them. I knew what they were. You could make out facial features, arms, and torsos.

They were all over. It appeared that there were two of them to one of us. Some were looking at the speaker talking. Others were looking at the people. And still others were weaving in and out, taking more than a passing interest in the people present. I did not want them near me. I did not like the energy that they came with and did not want them to know I existed. I went even deeper into myself and called upon my angels to phase me out, just enough to make them not see me. The pain became unbearable then. It was then that some of my energies began to leak into their realm. It most likely sounds strange to you, and I have to admit, so far it's a tough pill to swallow myself.

I don't remember much of the talk. My energies were spent observing these alien grays go about their business, knowing as each second passed that my wall of protection was getting weaker and the pain was increasing. I did not know how much more of it I could take. It was interesting to see people sitting around listening to an alien talk without the knowledge that they were actually there.

About ninety percent into this situation I noticed that in the areas where the pain was intense, a stream of energy was being drawn out from my body through the veil that shielded me from their eyes and into the out-of-phase areas where they were. The stream kept getting worse. The rate of energy flow kept getting larger. Eventually I noticed a couple of them sense this new energy being emitted. They turned around, looking backward and forward.

At first they did not notice me. I became alarmed. Had I been found out? Did I want them to know that I knew they were there? What should I do? I decided to act like I did not notice them. What they did not know I felt was to my advantage. I knew I was protected, but I still did not want them to visit me at night. Finally, after what seemed like twenty seconds of searching, two of them, with their eyes slightly widened, noticed me for the first time since they were there and came up to me. One of them put his face about six inches from mine. It was hard to look through a transparent, slightly out-of-phase alien and act like I did not see it.

I was relieved when the talk was over. I was in a lot of pain—more pain than I had been in for the entire week. I was drained and exhausted. I felt I could not move. Weakened from this experience. I was happy to see them slowly disappear. Then the fog went. And finally the old archangel energy reappeared. That was when I heard someone ask the group if anyone else had noticed the grays were here.

I had never put much stock into the existence of extra terrestrials. I believed they existed, but have always felt that they were not my battle to wage. I had enough on my plate with the energies and visits from angels, guides, spirits, archangels, and multi-dimensional beings without adding another group to my plate. I knew what I saw was the truth even if I did not fully understand the experience of it.

25

A Blessing or a Curse

As I have explained on numerous times in the earlier chapters of this book, I have the ability to sense many energy patterns on various levels. This was not always the case. I grew up understanding bits and pieces of the order of the universe but didn't know what energy signatures, tonal vibrations, and vibrational waves were. Nor did I understand how they interact with each other and their effects they have into this physical realm.

This knowledge became a by-product of my earlier training. Not realizing what I was developing and literally becoming, I started out in life knowing fragments of past lives, sensing spirits and angels. I didn't have the ability to sense energy shifts as I do now. My main goal was to find the Divine God light. I wanted to move into his energy and feel what he felt like, to be absorbed by his energy, to feel complete once again. I felt compelled and drawn to this goal. Through this journey I have found my place in the universe. I felt acceptance in my understanding of it and how it interacts with everything else.

While such experiences aren't constant, there are just enough of these events in my day to serve as a constant reminder of how things have changed. I find it both exhilarating and troubling at the same time. Thoughts of others weigh down upon my shoulders and pile up upon each other till I feel like I'm about to break. Imagine that when you hear what people talk, you feel it on multiple levels. I hear what they're physically saying. In the same wavelength I also feel the energy wave of the state of mind they're in, and on occasion I also hear what they're thinking. It becomes trying at times sorting out all three inputs.

If a person's state of mind is pleasant and their words are lighthearted, the energy wave they give off lifts you into a positive state of mind. When you hear someone's voice and they talk pleasantly enough but the energy they emit is under stress or they themselves are going through unpleasant events, you feel the waves of energy hitting you, slicing into your energetic self. These feel like hundreds of superficial wounds. The more you care about this person, the more deeply the cut is and the more the pain is felt.

The following is only one of many examples I can give. On this occasion my specialist physician, whom I have been seeing for years, had moved her practice elsewhere. I was in my new doctor's office waiting for this physician to go through the mounds of test results. As he spoke of continuing the same drugs as the previous doctor had, I also heard his mind telling me also that he was afraid of this drug and did not like the fact I was on it. The energy signature he gave off was one of apprehension.

Both his spoken word and what he was thinking became blended together, and because they were conflicting I became confused. After he finished, I looked at him and repeated what he thought, not what he said, and it was totally different than what he had verbally told me. He set down the papers. His eyes widened, and with his deer-caught-in-the-headlight look he asked me how did I know that he did not want me to continue with the current regimen. What do you tell him—"Yes, doctor I read your mind"? First of all, I don't. And secondly if I had that ability this chapter would not have been included in this book.

As I go through normal, day-to-day business I find I have to be very careful in understanding each individual section of thought I receive. I need to be consciously aware that what I'm hearing is categorized into thought and verbal voice. And lastly I have to make sure that I understand the wave of energy they emit and separate it from the first two.

This happens to me a lot in my work environment. I have meetings where people voice their thought or discuss the direction in which they want to proceed. I then get their thoughts on what their true intent is. And finally I get their energy wave emitting their frame of mind and whether their intent is misguided or not.

I find myself forgetting the spoken words and mixing in their thoughts as to the direction in which they want to precede. This has gotten me into some interesting circumstances. If I'm not careful, I find myself heading down a path that has not been discussed. To reduce this to a minimum I find myself repeating what has transpired when people speak so I can eliminate any confusion into what they themselves are saying.

This does play on my emotions as well. I start to read into things and wonder if certain people are using me for their own goals. I begin to see patterns, try to understand them. These feelings are grouped into an organized train of thought. Then when I have enough data I try to make a judgment call as to whether this person is trying to use me or if it is just in their makeup. Are they being a true friend or just being there to fulfill another purpose?

My emotions are on a roller coaster at times. Instead of trying to shut it down, I find myself going deeper to see if I can intercept the energy wave farther ahead, allowing me to deflect it slightly so as to affect the outcome in this physical realm. I have an engineering type of mind. I don't like to show my emotions, keeping them closely guarded. So when I have to deal with the emotions that the thoughts and energy waves are giving off, I find it trying at times. The spoken word does not have the same affect on me. It's the other two areas that do.

The worse emotional effect in dealing with these three areas is when I do find myself opening up my inner self, exposing my soft underbelly and ripping off my hard, outer, protective shell. When I have on occasion found someone that on some level has an interest in me, those energy waves are the most intense. When this happens the first time, the spoken word and thought somehow takes a back seat in the exchange. My mind processes this energy wave and interprets it as the combining of all three areas.

It takes a while to realize that what I feel and hear is not what is actually being spoken but instead is their higher self relaying to me things that the individual does not consciously realize. I find myself acting upon these energy waves. Through the interaction in the physical realm I tend to find out very quickly that what I interpreted was not a mutual exchange.

Keep in mind I'm talking about subtle things here. Because I have opened myself up, it feels like a gaping wound. The emotions go haywire. On a physical level it is not noticed, but on a spiritual level it becomes damaging to my emotional state. This of course is a lesson I'm still trying to overcome and adapt to.

And finally the last aspect in these three areas is that once energy has been exchanged—and I'm referring to a higher vibration energy wave—I feel the pushing– pulling effect it has on my own emotional state. If there is on some level an exchange of energy I become charged by it. I feel more complete. This could happen once, twice, or multiple times. Each time, I find myself anticipating the next meeting.

It becomes painful when on occasion I meet this person and they themselves are dealing with their own problems of life; I feel that emptiness. I feel the absence of the energy that I'd become accustomed to. I have known when friends were beginning to change direction in their life and start to pull away. It feels like a loss of sorts. It becomes a scarring inside—almost like a piece of me has been cut away. I have not learned how to make this easier. Each time it happens, it is still as painful as the first time it happened.

Is this a blessing or a curse? I think both. I could not even consider living life without this ability, and at the same token I wonder how I can deal with another interaction and the pain I feel with each loss. I've come to find that both the good and bad events that transpire in my life always have a higher purpose, though at the time and sometimes even many years later it is unclear what that purpose is.

However, some answers do trickle down and become known. It has not been an easy life. Trying to work on so many levels simultaneously and maintain some sort of coherency between them is a process I find at times to be almost impossible.

26

I'm Not Worthy Enough for His Love

There are events in life that when they come about you wonder why you were allowed such a wonderful gift. As you have read in the beginning of this book, I do remember fragments of my life with Jesus. I do remember following him through his teachings when he was down here.

These events and many more I yearn to remember in greater detail. I knew what his energetic self feels like. I knew what his intent was, and I understood what his true teachings were—at least as they related to my place in this universe. I remember his gatherings on other realms and planes of existence.

I can remember that on multiple occasions I had the honor to have a visit from this holy and wonderful man. For each of these events I was transported to another reality. These were not dreams. They were as real as this physical world. Whenever I jump into these realms, memories of past visits starts to string together into my memory.

The only way I can describe it is as living in one, continuous, running movie, and I make appearances throughout it. And many times I can remember the prior visits that had happened in months, years and decades past. I can draw upon these memories as you would in the physical world and use them in the current visit. Let me state right here that these are not dreams. They are real planes of existence that exist out of phase with our reality. When I'm there I can feel the dirt, the trees, and even other people. The textures are as real as anything you feel here.

I have had the honor to have Christ visit me on a few occasions in the first half of my life. There were a series of visits that contained the same series of events in my teen years and one major event in my earlier twenties. I came from these visits changed. He is one of the spirits that on some level always stays with me. I never understood why he would find me worthy enough to allow these events to occur. I am thankful that he graced me with them.

The first series of events were spread across my teen years. They happened within eight months to a few years apart. They were all similar in nature with the exception of the distance away from Christ I had been in each vision. They all started out the same. I was either sitting in a chair or lying on the bed. This of course was not in the house I was living at but instead in one particular farmhouse.

The season was winter. The first couple of times it happened the leaves had fallen off the trees and lay scattered around the ground. Frost covered everything. In the first visit I got out of bed feeling like something had been outside. I remember the boards creaking as I walked over to the window to look out.

I can remember looking into the woods that just lay a couple of yards past my window and noticing a hooded man within the middle of these woods with his hands down by his side stretched outward toward me. As we stared at each other, my body became immobilized and could not move away from the window. I was not afraid; I knew who he was even though I could not see his face at this time.

I did not understand what he wanted. And to this day I can speculate but I don't fully understand why. No words were spoken. I felt his emotional thought that he wanted to talk to me. He also kept pressing upon me that he was waiting patiently for me to come out.

This vision was repeated for me on many occasions as years passed, with one minor change in each. In each vision, Jesus moved closer to the window and farther out of the woods. The seasons slightly changed also. I noticed that fall had come and gone and winter was upon us.

The last of these types of trips had me waking into this reality in the chair in the living room. Again I was in the same old farmhouse. I knew who was outside so I rushed to the front door. I told myself no more looking at him in the window. As I opened the door and stepped out, a slight dusting of snow had settled down upon the ground, covering the leaves and branches.

I went over to the woods to see. I stopped about fifteen feet from him. He had his hood off. We stood there staring at each other. With his arms outstretched no words were spoken. Many unspoken words passed from his mind to mine. Changes I had felt were beginning to melt into myself and work deeply into my being. I did not want to leave. I wanted to know what he wanted from me. What did he want me to do? I wanted to tell him that I loved him and would do anything he asks of me. As hard as I tried, I could not speak. I just stared at him as he looked calmly back at me.

The last time I had a visit from him was when I was in my early twenties. This was one of the most intense visits I have had. It was in the early stages of my quest to find out who I was and where I needed to go. During this time in my life I felt like I had the spiritual rope dragging me along this path of self-discovery. Feeling great amounts of inadequacy at the progress

I was making, I thought I was wasting not only my time but God's as well.

My mind was in turmoil sorting out not only this lifetime's experiences but flashes of past lives and time on the other sides. Every time I reviewed my efforts, I always felt I came up short on the subject. I felt like I never quite matched up to anything.

This trip started with me in a reality that I was familiar with, but the scenery was different. I was standing on what looked like an asphalt road. Looking down this highway I was amused to see that it was straight for as far as my eye could see. I started to walk down it.

It felt like I had been walking for a small period of time when I noticed off in the distance that the highway I was on ended at another road that was perpendicular to the one I was on. When I got to the T-intersection, on each side of both roads there stood tall pine trees. The forest was so dense you could only look a couple of feet past the beginning of the first set of trees.

The sky was gray. I looked down toward my left and noticed the road headed straight for miles with trees on each side. On the right the road looked like it headed into a clearing of sorts. So I decided out of curiosity to take a right and to follow this paved road to see where it led.

I came upon a clearing. At first I saw what looked like a small lumber village. Shacks were scattered all around the edge of the clearing. As I walled through this town I could not find anyone. I knew people had been there because of the items that lay around. It was almost as if they suddenly stopped for some important event. Then I noticed it: off to one of the sides of the clearing in a field stood the townsfolk, all gathered around something. I walked toward them. Wanting to find out what the commotion was about, I pushed myself through this crowd toward the center. As I broke through the last remaining group of people I noticed that Jesus was on a wooden platform some distance from this crowd.

I desperately wanted to be next to him. So without asking I walked calmly up to him and sat down at his feet on his right side. Looking around at the crowd I saw the expressions on the faces of these villagers. They wore expressions of awe and fear. I said out loud, "Come closer. This man has traveled far." Then Jesus spoke to me. He said that these people would come closer as they developed.

Each person's evolution would take him or her back to the Divine. There was no set time to accomplish this, and everyone would reach the same destination at one point or another. Jesus then said he approved of me remaining seated next to him and also that I could stay there as long as I liked. I felt like a kid then, looking up upon this man with wondrous awe and beauty and listening to his words harmonizing with all that had ears to hear.

After a time I became impatient, as a kid does when they want a parent to notice them. To accomplish this, they first start with small gestures and slowly increase their efforts to be noticed by doing larger things. I was no different. I tugged on his robes and waited. He kept talking. I tugged again, and again nothing. Then the third time I tugged really hard. I wanted him to notice me, not that crowd. After all, I came up and sat next to him—they did not.

Then he stopped talking. Looking down at me as a parent with an angry look, he stared at me. Through a mind's connection a link had been formed. The flood of fears and things that were troubling me flooded into his mind. Then I heard his voice. He sternly asked me then should he listen to me—ignore these people who waited to hear him speak and instead give him his undivided attention to my petty problems? Then he looked back into the crowd. He started back up from where he had been interrupted.

I remember coming awake then into in my bed in complete shame. I cried. It took me many months to get over the shame of what I had done. And it took me many years to understand what the true message was about.

This event changed me. I found myself caught up in my own problems that I had amplified and stretched into something that had taken a life of its own. I did not realize the true gifts that were being given to me. I have never received a visit again in my life from Jesus.

I have on occasion received a message from some mediums. They would start to cry and began to tell me that Jesus had spoken to them. They would tell me that it had never happened before. I do know he is still taking an active role in the Divine plan that has been chosen for me, though I still do not understand the full extent of it.

27

They Did Help with My Memory

It always amazes me how when things start to change, your mind does not comprehend any movement. I had an opportunity to look back upon my path and notice that I have walked great distances. I am not the same person I was weeks, months, or even years ago.

We all change, but I have felt that the changes I have gone through in the last couple of years in some ways could measured by leaps and bounds. I have told you before that I do get visits from dimensional beings. This is no secret. I totally don't understand were they come from or what exact role they play in the evolution of our planet. I have come to accept that they are not extraterrestrials but high-level beings from a plane of existence out of phase from our own. It took me many years to accept this answer. I do know that their energy signatures are unique. I also know they come close to this physical realm when great changes are being made in our evolution.

This story begins at a gathering I had at my place. A group of my friends had gotten together as we normally do. A knock at the door was heard. I got up from my chair like I have done hundreds of times before, using my arms as leverage. On my right hand I heard a loud crack. Everyone stopped talking and looked over. The back of my hand turned blood red and spread across the backside down toward my fingers. Within seconds the skin appeared to dry out with crack-like formations across it.

I still had movement, but the discomfort became a continuous pain. Paying little attention to it the rest of the night, thinking I would feel better the next day, I went off to sleep. I woke up with my right hand swollen and discolored, but I knew I could move my fingers and figured it wasn't broken. I did not want to spend the expense or time of heading off to an urgent care center for attention. I asked my angels if I should go. I heard them say that everything be all right.

The discomfort became worse as the day went on. I tried to not move my hand or use it through the working day. When I got home I wrapped it up in a bandage and figured it would be ok. After a little while the bandage became tight so I removed it. My hand had swollen even larger, so I asked my angels again should I get it checked out. I heard from them two answers. First of all they said everything would be all right. Then they said if you want the truth to be known go to the urgent care. I figured that what they meant was I could find out whether it was broken or not. So I decided to get it checked out.

The doctor told me after looking at it that he did not think any bones were broken, but he figured that the loud popping noise came from the gases in the knuckles. He wanted me to get an x-ray of it anyway. I was sitting in a little room when one of the x-ray technicians came in and asked me if I was here because of the metal chip that they had found. I looked at her dumbfounded. I said I had no chip. She then replied that I did.

The doctor came back to me minutes later and asked if I was in any pain. I replied to him that it hurt but that was to be expected from the damage I did the day before. He then said to me that he was referring to the metal chip in my right hand. I asked him to show me this x-ray. The location of this metal chip was on the backside of my hand above the bone of the thumb located down toward the wrist. He then proceeded to tell me he did not understand why I would not remember such a large metal chip being inserted into me. I replied that I was not experiencing any pain and don't know how this had happened. Then my mind phased into two. As he was asking me all sorts of weird questions, I felt his mind's thoughts. He did not believe that this was a normal metal chip.

He was trying to understand how it related to a medical explanation. I then heard from my angels that it was an implanted chip. I thought to myself there were two types of implants. Was it from an extraterrestrial, or did one of the doctors insert this chip during one of my many surgeries? The doctor then asked me if he could forward my x-ray images to a specialist for further evaluation.

I got home that night realizing what my angels had meant about me knowing the truth. I had thought they were talking about the bone being broken or not. They instead wanted me to understand that I had an implant. I asked my angels again, whether I should be concerned. They replied that it was a good thing to have it in my body. The very next day I surfed the Internet trying to find images of implants in people's hands. I did find a few of them with chips in the exact location that my chip was.

I relayed the story about what had happened to a few friends that Saturday at a convention I was attending. The very next day a good friend of mine came up to me and said she had heard of my implant and proceeded to tell me about a message she had gotten. She said that it came from dimensional beings. I had not told her at that time of my experience with these beings. There were only a few people that knew about them. This of course gave me a confirmation of what I suspected.

A couple of weeks later a friend of mine was channeling and spoke of my implant contained within my right hand. The being that was within her spoke of this chip as being a device that helps me keep my focus and my thumb on things. Then it hit me. It was like pieces of the puzzle falling down into the correct order and forming a picture. I remember that in the last six months my memory has gotten better. I am remembering more of my day-to-day events. Time has seemed to stabilize, and I have been able to concentrate with greater focus and intent than I have been able to in many years. It was a gradual thing. I do remember that within a very short time my mental state had returned to level of normalcy

If it weren't for the interactions I have had over the years with these dimensional beings as well as messages I have gotten from different friends, I would have logically chalked it up to a sliver moving slowly from the palm of my hand toward the back. But with all the mounting evidence and hearing my angels' voices, I could not deny that it was placed there by other means. All I truly know is that I do remember better. Even though I still don't remember my past or even many events in my life, I am more centered in this reality. It appears to be like an anchor, rooting me more on this plane.

28

Did We Get It Wrong?

Out of all the chapters I have written and of all the things I said, I find what I'm about to express on paper to be one of the most explosive topics. I have opened myself up and exposed my vulnerability in the previous chapters, but they have not caused as much controversy as this one will.

I sat here a long time trying to find the right words to portray this hidden truth in such a way as not to cause uproar or disbelief. This is what I believe as the true nature of what we are. I'm not trying to push any type of idea or goals upon anyone. If this rings true in your mind, then please take the best pieces and make them your own. If not, then understand that these ideas are mine and accept them for what they are.

Have you ever watched your favorite movie multiple times? You understand the sequence of events that transpire within the movie. You know what will happen next. Some of you might even know the words that each actor will say. There comes a time, and it may take a few nights of watching the same movie over and over, when a light flashes in your mind.

There is something about the movie, an undertone, that you have never noticed before. It could be the foundation of the entire plot or it could be a personality of a character or two. You say to yourself, why didn't I notice this before? I say to you the timing wasn't right. You needed to watch this movie time and time again till your level of awareness shifted to a point that you were allowed to view it with a deeper understanding of what it was really meant to be.

After this epiphany you view the same movie with different eyes. The whole plot changes. A new awareness begins to develop. And you are slightly changed by this experience. Even though the movie itself has not changed, you move from one state of awareness into another. You are changed to a slight degree, and then each time after you view this movie you see it with new eyes.

Now imagine this movie as being the life you live. Each time you view this movie of life you come down upon this physical realm and experience the plot. Yes, I'm talking about not living only one life but many times. You see this life as your conscious self—viewing each segment as the movie unfolds. Each time you sit down to view this movie you come into a new life with a predetermined set of experiences you need to experience.

You change the plot slightly each time this movie is played in order to gain the experience and understanding your higher self needs to expand. Each time you sit down in the beginning to watch, you change characters. One time you're the hero. Another time you're the villain, and at times you're the character who has only a few lines. We all experience every role in this movie at one time or another.

There comes a time in your development when you begin to realize that it's not the character itself that our divine soul is trying to grow but instead the hidden meaning between each frame of the movie itself. Once this inspired epiphany is realized, the movie itself changes—or at least the view you have of it. When this happens, you cannot go back into that dull lull of sleep and live through it, playing your part as it once was meant to be. You become awakened from your slumber. Your divine self calls to you, and you have no choice but to follow.

If you have found this book, by means of a friend or family member, then I say to you that this book has found you. There is a piece of your divine self that has on some level awakened and seen something that your conscious self has not been aware of. Your divine self is calling you, and you need to become aware of what path it needs. There is no turning back. You need to change your role in this divine movie of life. You need to become empowered with the Divine God. The spark has been ignited, and it needs to grow.

Before this world became into being, we all sat down on the other side and wanted a place where we could experience ideas, thoughts, and processes with a freedom of will. We wanted to be stripped away and broken down from our divine self and the Divine God within, to be shoved down into a movie and to experience it as we were intended to.

This has never been done like this in the universe before, and luckily this plan became a huge success. Through hardships and diversity, pieces of ourselves were allowed to not only grow and develop by leaps and bounds but also to find the Divine God hidden within everything.

So we set up subplots within this epic movie. Each segment is drastically different, allowing us to experience different pieces of the puzzle. This allows each one of us to find the truth behind God and our role within that truth. On the other side, each of us knows the truth. On this plane of existence we need to keep striving with each different character. We need to experience this forced separation from God until we realize how to find what we're looking for. There is no rule as to how many times it takes in reviewing this movie of life before we come to this conclusion. We all reach it at some time.

At first we live lifetime after lifetime with the understanding, on some level, that we seek to be whole again. We search with each character, knowing on some level that the Divine God that has been removed from our consciousness. With each experience we gain a piece of awareness on where to look.

When we exhaust every potential, we come to the realization that God is not external but that instead the true path of enlightenment is within. Most people will agree with me on this, but if you look closely at what they say you see differently. When most people pray they pray for an external Divine intervention. For this is what we have been taught lifetime after lifetime, seeking out a spiritual help from priests, rabbis, or monks. When we pray to God, our intent is to pray to an external source.

These are all outward actions in searching for something that is not external but instead is hidden internally within ourselves. We must realize that what we have consciously lost is not gone but only out of sight.

We are all part of the Divine God. As God came into existence by thought alone, his essence is not that of a complete being but instead is made up of innumerable individual sparks of light. Each individual spark grows by the direct results of each experience that has been directed toward its developing consciousness. Because each spark desires to express itself, there are no two alike.

At some time in history these Divine sparks of God light wanted to develop their consciousness. At this point in time it was decided as a whole to accomplish this task by setting themselves into an epic movie of life, in which they would repeat each character to better understand the role of God and themselves within the body of God itself.

We are those sparks of light. The Divine God is hidden within each one of us. Every spark, with its entirety, makes up the body of God. This being is not outside, lost from us. We have not been removed from his light because of any sin we have or our father or grandfather has done. We are the Divine being, at least a piece of him. We need to look within for guidance.

Do not misunderstand what I'm saying. I'm not separating myself from God by saying that we are God, but instead what I'm telling you is that by accepting the Divine God within, we are accepting the true power of God. It is in everything, and by drawing upon the Divine spark within we in turn stand in the presence of God himself.

The human race has gone as far as it can with the current state of understanding. Many people are misinterpreting the changes the millennium has brought about. They think them as the end of days. In some ways it is. It is the end of days for the current understanding of what God is and how we play in his divine plan. We all are growing.

We are developing a level of awareness that what we are currently doing is not working. We are coming to a realization that what we seek is not located on the outside of us but instead that the true path is within each of us. We need not only seek within ourselves but to seek it as well with the full knowledge that we are pieces of the Divine. We are all God, even if we can feel only a piece of him.

The first step in any new path is recognizing the new ideas and concepts. Then we have to review it within our own belief structure. We need to remove those ideas that no longer suit our needs. Then finally we need to push off into the new direction to test those new concepts, accepting what feels like truth and disregarding what does not. We need to start training ourselves.

The times when we sit down to commune with God, we need to set the intent by going within ourselves. We need to feel his presence by piercing on a quantum level through the core of every atom within our body, pulling this Divine God self through and allowing it to shine into this realm within.

Becoming one again with our higher God self, we also become one with the God selves of everyone. As we start to notice others with the same degree as we do with ourselves, then we start to get a larger picture of God himself.

29

The Next Stage in Development

Before coming into any lifetime, our Divine self sets up the role we need to play. Reviewing what its higher cosmic self wishes to express and learn from, your Divine self sets up the good and bad events that are needed to reach each experienced outcome. Though we have free will to change any part of this outline, these trials will be pressed upon our life in varying degrees.

Our Divine self needs certain experiences to allow itself to grow and expand. In order to accomplish its goal, the higher self sets up an outline then sends a piece of us down into this movie to play the role we had designed for ourselves, with all its good and bad. It's the learning from each experience that builds upon itself to form who and what we are. We add to the collection of the whole.

On the other side we decided the best way to gain the most experience is to split a part of ourselves off from the Divine God Self and play a part in the movie of life—to forget our true self for a moment in time, spending lifetime after lifetime in search of the truth. We decided to set things up so we could feel what it is like to know that something is missing and hidden from us. In order to accomplish this we set up a protective veil that separates this physical reality from the other side.

I like to think that chakras are thin areas of the veil. I think the location of the veil that each of us have is located on a quantum level between the nucleus of each atom. For demonstration purposes let's imagine a person standing straight up. Behind this person is a thin fog-like membrane. And behind it is the Divine God light. The Divine light hits this veil.

This membrane acts like a prism of sorts. It divides the light and sends it into the areas that have the thinnest point in the veil, allowing a color type to filter through. Now imagine these thin points of the veil are the areas of the chakras. Each chakra allows a single color to shine through. This design was intended as the best way to filter the Divine light into this physical realm and still allow a stable flow of energy. Our minds were not ready and could not handle a more purified form of God energy.

We are in a critical stage of development as a whole in humanity. We have come as far as we can with the current state of mindset. In order to grow, develop, and learn new ideas and concepts, we need to change the energy itself to allow a different Divine flow. This next stage in development is rewiring this veil. By moving the body, as illustrated in the paragraph above, so the veil runs along the center of each chakra, we in turn cancel out the effects of the veil. The prism no longer is needed, and the Divine light energy flows freely and consistently into this reality. By changing our concept of an external God and living each moment as part of the Divine God, we change the intent and the flow of energy itself.

I have found that for me the best way to allow this change is to keep correcting my intent to focus my prayers and conscious state to be drawing from within the Divine God self. Up to this point in human development we could not see our Divine self because of this veil. But with this change in consciousness we are allowing a change to the rules that govern this membrane itself.

You can see your own divine self. There is a way: by changing the flow of energy and allowing the light to not to be limited to the thin point in the veil, not be limited to the locations of each chakra. Instead of using the nucleus of each atom and reaching through it on a quantum level, you are allowed to grab pieces of your own divine self and pull them through into this realm. Each time this process is done, the hole gets larger and the flow of energy becomes more constant. The need for chakras become less and less.

The idea behind this new development is to become Christ-like. He was able to pull his divine self through each atom and in turn his body became one giant chakra. His body became a complete, individual vortex of Divine energy, bringing forth God into this physical reality.

As we start to walk in this new way of thinking, our intent changes. The old rules that govern flows of energy become void. They no longer apply or have an effect upon our change state. We take back our Divine selves and truly become masters of our own reality. We become creators within this physical reality, molding energies using the Divine light and bringing heaven upon this earth. This is not magic. Nor is it demonic.

This is the true gift that was given to each of us when our sparks of light were created. It may take generations of people to fully develop this state of awareness, but it is possible to grasp portions of it within your own lifetime. Expand your mind to accept what at first seems like abstract concepts, draw them into your reality, and make them a part of you.

Since the new millennium the mind state in every human being has grown and changed. Some have adapted to this very well, and still others have not. We as a race are becoming and evolving into a higher level of being. The mind is expanding to allow ideas and concepts that seemed too bizarre only a few years ago to create a plausible set of rules that will govern our lives.

We as a whole will be shifting our state of mind to no longer look externally for the Divine but instead recognize it within. We will be accepting the true power that each of us has denied. This will open up on many different levels for each of us. It will allow us to truly experience what God is and how we are a part of him. We will begin to see the Divine God not only in others but also in every living thing. We will see what parts each of them plays in our role in this movie of life.

With this expansion of our awareness and realization of the power of the Divine God in each of us, we will begin to work with energies and realities to mold and manifest them upon this physical realm in ways that very few have ever accomplished before. We will be able not only to understand multiple realities and planes of existence but to move freely between them. We will be able to tap into the other side and talk to our loved ones, angels, and guides. Imagine having the ability to feel that we are not alone, to tap into pieces of ourselves and follow that golden thread through each part of us till we reach our cosmic self.

We are all like icebergs floating in a great sea. Only a small fraction of every thought and action manifests itself upon this physical reality. An iceberg is no different; what you see on the surface of the water does not truly show the full extent of this floating chunk of ice. We can only understand a small portion of our full Divine self. Humankind is developing to be able not only to sense what lies underneath the surface but to have the ability to see it as well. Each of us will discover that we have not lost God. Our conscious selves allowed our whole being to be submerged under the depths of the sea to hide the full extent of who we are and the Divine within. This was to remain hidden till each of us have evolved to a point that we could see clearly enough and understand it for what it really is.

30

The Divine Self, Cosmic Self, and God

In my feeble attempts in trying to sketch out a concept of my understanding of what God is and my role in his grand design, I have found that it has not been an easy one. I can only hope I can relay a small portion of this grand idea and form in words a structure that can be easily understood and absorbed on a conscious level. As I reach deeper into the mire of who God is, I realize that the journey has been a long and strenuous one. After decades of searching far and wide I finally came home and discovered that to find the answers I sought, I need never have left.

They were there right in front of my eyes, if I had only shifted my thinking. Was I wrong in heading out trying to find what I sought? I think not. Sometimes the journey itself allows you to reach a mindset that will be most compatible when the nourishment is obtained. I truly don't think I would have appreciated the level of understanding if I had not done what I did in this life.

Let's take a look at God himself. As I have already described earlier in this book, God is made up of a numerable collection of Divine sparks. As these sparks develop a consciousness they transform into the Divine self. Through the sheer desire to express themselves, they build layer upon layer of consciousness. A personality forms and molds its development as each experience is absorbed and understood. When you shift this molded spark out of time and space into a place where there is no past, present, or future and yet they exist simultaneously at once, you get the cosmic self. This being is a collection of all the experiences and expressions of its soul—a completed being. This cosmic self is the accumulation of what we were, are, and will become.

When you look at stories of near-death experiences they talk about seeing God at the end of the tunnel. With its sheer beauty and magnificence, this vision is understood to be God himself. The people who've had these experiences are not wrong in their assumption, but they are not totally correct either. This is truly God, but not in the sense that we humans want to view him as. This high-level being is our own cosmic self looking back at us, accepting a piece of itself back into the fold. Keep in mind the cosmic self exists outside of space and time. For it knows what you have lived, are living, and yet need to experience.

When the Divine self desires a set of experiences to learn and grow, it works with the cosmic self to set up situations in other realities and planes of existences. The cosmic self splits along with the Divine self and sends pieces to realms that will best enable them to experience what they need. This is the dividing of ourselves into different areas of realities and eventually down upon this physical realm. It splits its higher self into a spirit. This part of you insures that you remain on track and helps the connection between each part of yourself. Then the spirit splits again and develops the soul. This section of yourself aids in the subconscious and dream state to form its necessary tasks. The soul splits once again and finally inhabits a body with a conscious mind-state.

Because we are moving into realities that maintain a linear time frame, we perceive ideas and concepts in past, present and future. Because of this physical realm, reality events are laid out in a linear fashion, allowing us to perceive lessons as journeys. When you perceive it on a cosmic level you are actually living many linear time frames in many different realities at the same time.

This brings me to the concept of God. For I truly believe there is a God, but it took me many lifetimes to understand a clear truth about what God is to me. First, take the idea that we are a part of the Divine God, a group of individual sparks that have personalities wrapped up upon itself. Now reach through your conscious mind down through your soul, going even farther down into the spirit and up through the Divine self till you can branch off and reconnect every Divine spark within the body of God. This body is the collection of everyone's cosmic being and every cosmic energy all wrapped up together. A sum total of everything and everyone linked together creates the mind of God.

I would like to go a little bit deeper into the energies that make up the core of God himself. Our cosmic self contains all past, present, and future events. It exists outside of space and time. Its core contains three basic elements. These elements are created and built from all our experiences, reactions, and actions. The first is the actual vibration of every element within our thoughts. It is the whole of every life on this and the other side as well as life on other worlds and planes of realities. The second set is the unique color we emit. And last is the sound we produce from the other two combined. As we obtain that state of bliss with the connection of the Divine God, we resonate with our entire being. This state of blissful sound is interpreted throughout the ages as angelic singing.

31

So That's What I Sound Like

I have had the blessing on two occasions in my life to experience not only the resonating sounds of my Divine self but to hear the harmonization of every Divine soul singing in unison. The joy of hearing my cosmic and Divine self—resonating with its whole essence—words fail to describe. As if that would not be joyous enough in itself, then I had the opportunity to hear my sound combining with other cosmic beings. For I truly know what was meant when the Bible talks about the chorus of angels singing.

I feel like a man traveling back in time four thousand years and explaining what a personal computer is. I can only hope that I am able to extract a piece of these experiences and allow my words to express what transpired.

Both times that I heard these harmonies occurred when I was in my twenties. The first time was in the beginning of my journey, and the second happened toward the end of my quest. Either experience in itself was a blessing and honor, but to experience it twice I felt exuberant. It took me many years to truly understand the depth of what had transpired. I find myself on occasion wishing I could capture just a portion of it, hoping that by doing so I can reconnect once again with my cosmic self.

As most of my visions seem to start out, I came conscious of myself in a wooden, earth-filled dwelling. I quickly realized that this event I was experiencing was a dream but was as real as anything can be. I opened up the door and walked out. As I stepped into the sunlight I noticed that I had a long, white, flowing robe on extending down to the ground, covering my feet. This robe contained strips of multi-colored bands running along the front and down each arm. Then it hit me—I realized that this was not a robe but my body.

There was nothing underneath it but light itself. I was first surprised then amazed at this. It did not take long before I noticed that there were rows of various sized dwellings running both up and down the dirt road that ran past the building I'd been in. As I looked around I noticed out of each dwelling there came an individual.

They were various shapes and sizes with different types of ethnic backgrounds. They were all walking toward a road that intersected all the dwellings. Everyone had a single-minded purpose. I felt drawn and compelled to follow. I knew I was a stranger here, and yet at the same time it felt home to me.

When we all reached the street we lined up in a row. They all turned to me then. As I walked down the path toward the outskirts of town, I heard in my mind that they were waiting for me to lead them up the path into the mountains. Not knowing what was going on and not wanting to upset them, I did what they asked. This place felt as real and vivid as living upon planet Earth. I did what they told me and went to the front of the procession.

I stood there looking past the outskirts of the town and watched the path wind itself up upon the single mountain that stood before me. What happen then I have never had happen to me before. I looked down at my folded hands. Pieces of my hand started to mold something upward, as if I was clasping something. When this image started to form I then realized it was a white candle.

Details on the surface of this newly formed candle became clear, as the form started to take shape. Then it finished, and a light started on the candle itself. I stood there in amazement. Looking around, I noticed that every person behind me had done the same thing. Each one of them was holding a lighted candle and waited calmly for me to start the precession.

We all strode silently out of the town heading toward the mountain. An interesting thing happened then. As we reached the base of this mountain they all began to sing. It was the most beautiful thing I had ever heard. Words could not come close to portray even a small portion of what it was. Such joy and wonderment each sound contained. I strained my ears but could not make out the words.

It took me a moment to realize that they were not words but the sound of their higher self vibrating, mixing with their unique color, and emitting it outward. As each wave hit and mixed with another it amplified this wondrous tone. Each persons vibration resonated, sent outwards and then combined together as a whole. I could not do anything but get caught up with the joy I was experiencing. As each wave of sound hit my body, I saw a pulse of light flair up within myself.

I continued to lead this group of spirits up toward the top of the mountain. Feeling my body rise with every second of each sound wave, I started to become aware of my own sound. It was small at first. As pulsating light grew within me, it became stronger. The higher I went up the more attuned with it I became. I felt small compared to the whole of the group but not separated from it. I felt like I was a part of them. Adding each sound I emitted into the singing of the group, I became not only more attuned to the sound from the whole but to my individual tone as well. I thought it interesting after this had ended that I could feel both separate sounds and yet they had seemed as one complete whole.

About twenty feet from the top of the mountain the procession stopped. The singing kept on. I was told that I had to reach the top alone, so I went the rest of the way. When I got to the top, there was only a small, flat surface that only one person could stand on. Keep in mind, I'm afraid of heights. But at this moment I was not. I looked down then. Rotating my view three hundred sixty degrees around this mountain, I notice the trail was filled with sound-emitting, loving spirits. They all filled the path that extended down to the base of this mountain.

I felt it then; a sudden surge of energy and light filled my entire being. It was the most intense experience I have ever felt. Looking down on myself I saw the bright white glow emitting brighter and brighter from inside my body; it began shining through the robe I wore. I looked up into the sky then, feeling the full presence of the Divine God himself. My body changed then. It turned to the brightest, most purified white you can possibly imagine. All external senses were lost.

All I felt was my cosmic self singing with all its might. The connection to God and everything was complete. I was one with everything and everyone. And though I thought it could not get better, the sound became alive in itself. It sent the love, light, and peace along with each wave of energy I emitted. The emotions I felt I cannot explain. I only wish I could give each one of you a understanding of what I experienced and hope that from what I write here you believe that I had truly experienced this wondrous event.

I knew upon awaking that next morning that I had lived through an event that few had done. I thought I knew then the full extent of the meaning, but as usual I did not. It took me other milestones of understanding to truly comprehend what those pulsating sounds were, what had happen to my transfiguration, and most of all why it had happened to me. There are other events in my life that I could look at with a logical mind and say that what I experienced could be explained in a physical sense, but in this case I know it was Divinely sent.

My mind could not have made up even a portion of what I saw. I could not have imagined the detail and vividness of everything. Like a lot of things that flood the system with those wondrous feelings I became addicted to it on some level. I yearned to experience those experiences continuously. Of course I could not.

32

My Divine Self

Over the years I must have put on over 100,000 miles traveling back and forth by vehicle into the western part of the United States. I don't like to fly. Whenever possible I enjoy driving from place to place. It allows you to see things that are off the beaten path. I have found many interesting areas by trying a new route. The west for me has so many splendors. From multi-colored rock formations to American Indian ruins, I never get tired of them. So on this particular occasion I decided to see what the east side of the United States had to offer. When I ever head out on my vacation excursions, I don't plan anything. I might say to myself, *Let's see Colorado*, and I end up in Nevada. All I do plan for is the amount of money I have to spend and the time frame. Other than that, it's up in the air.

I figured I would travel around the edges of the eastern part of the United States and see what I could find. With no particular destination in mine I headed off. Everything was going fine until I reached New York State. As I have explained many times in previous chapters I deal with pain a lot. For me when I feel my pain and it is the same type of constant feeling, I do the best I can to block it out and go upon my daily business. It is only when the pain changes, and suddenly at that, that I get concerned. It started on my second day of this trip.

The pain in my abdomen became intense. It became a sharp, constant, stabbing pain. I became alarmed by it. I did not want to be admitted into an emergency room in a state where I knew no one. I asked myself, should I try to make it home or stay around a day or two to see if anything changes. I was afraid to make any long trip back, so I decided to stay in Rochester, New York.

I was traveling around trying to find a hotel that was near a hospital when I remembered my friend telling me a year prior that there was a convention being held in Rochester around the time I was there. Figuring I could at least have someone I knew be aware of what was happening I decided to find where it was being held and stay there a couple of days to see whether the pain got worse or better.

Little did I know at that time that this would be the best move I could make. After checking in I traced down the admission people and inquired as to the whereabouts of my friend. In the process I found out that I could sign up for day passes as a visitor and take part in the festivities. I said to myself this would be a good way to pass the time.

I have been to variations of these types of conventions in the past. Each one had a unique perspective about them. Some were better than others, but I have always found that I enjoyed them. Having an open mind about these things, I went into this one with as curious a mind as I could with my current state.

This convention, the International Spiritualist Federation, was not like the past ones I had attended. The members consisted of people all around the world coming together with a common interest. I was able to have my eyes opened to various types of ideas, healing modalities, and viewpoints. This in itself would have been worth spending the entire time there. But the events that followed shadowed them.

At this particular convention they had different types of classes that you could sign up for. Healing, medium-ship, and meditations were only a few. Not wanting to join a group already in progress with a topic I was not too familiar with, I decided to join the healing classes.

They had done a smart thing in this convention. Each series of classes on the same topic was held in the same room. This allowed the energies to build up upon themselves. I walked into the healing class. As I turned around the corner into the doorway it hit me all of a sudden. Not only did my pain increase three-fold but also the energies I felt were intense.

When I feel waves of energies in the air, it's like seeing ripples when a rock is tossed into a body of water. These waves feel like if you're in a pool and are walking from one end to another. You feel that resistance to them. In this case it felt like I was trying to push through mud.

My body responded to this new, intense energy, and my vibration started to increase. I knew at that time I could either accept this new energy and try to absorb its vibration rate and grow upon it or block these energies out. I knew that my increase in pain was the direct cause of this increase in energy. I resolved myself to the fact that I would either be admitted into the hospital in a couple of days or the energy itself would heal it.

It always is interesting to get together with a group of people that are sensitive to spirit and energy, for they pick up on things that most people do not see or feel. I walked around that week in an altered state. My aura I could see and feel expand out from my body three times its normal size. I would see it brighter, whiter, and refined. I have only experienced that a couple of times in my life. This usually came on when I was at my height of my journey in spirit.

My mind split into two realities, which was an ability I had lost a long time ago. I became conscious in two states at the same time. I lived that week both in this physical plane as well as my mind-state living in the spiritual reality. I was still dealing with the physical pain, but that no longer matter to me. Toward the end of this convention I started to feel the strain of maintaining both consciousnesses.

It started to tax my mind. When my mind splits if feels like I'm standing and conscious in two separate realities at the same time. Between these states I get the feeling like when you take Silly Putty and grab both ends, stretching it to the point of breaking. I feel both consciousnesses have that elastic resistance to them. They want to come back into one mindset. The only thing keeping them apart is sheer will.

That week not only attended the healing classes but I also received the laying on of hands. I experienced many different types of healing. I had total strangers come up to me and explain that they seen a massive amount of angels around me. Some would say that I had bright white light shining out from my body. I knew this was true because I was not only seeing it myself but was also feeling it.

I felt intense energy, light, and thousands of beings surrounding me. My split consciousness became aware of them, communed with them, and shared my energy with them. I found during that week that I needed twelve hours of sleep a day. I told myself that I would not worry about my pain and let things unwind as they were meant to.

As each day had passed, the energies inside the healing room became more and more intense. Time seem to slow down, or at the very least my perception of it did. I knew it was building up to some great climax, but I did not have a clue what that climax would be. That event arrived the second to the last day of the class. Having lived in both realities for days now in a dream-like state, my consciousness was open and ready to receive the unexpected.

We were doing a technique when you have a person sit in a chair with a photograph of someone they loved who needed healing. Everyone stood there circling around them with one hand on the person sitting there and another hand on a shoulder of someone next to them. We had three rows of people standing there. Being aware of my state I did not want to touch anyone, not knowing if something would happen so I stood in the back of the last row with my hands outstretched, pointing to the group. We closed our eyes and prayed.

Feeling the energy around me. I first focused upon the countless angels surrounding me. I felt their energy. I moved within them. I felt the increased energy within myself. I realized at that time I could use this moment to move through the nucleus of every atom. I could pierce the veil on a quantum level in order to see how far I could head toward my cosmic self.

I became the energy itself. I was conscious of my body, but to a larger degree I was more aware of my new state of mind. The light emitted from myself mixed with the beings around me, and I became aware of the tonal vibration of all our combined energies. The spark of God began to emerge. The sound being emitted grew larger. I was conscious of my personality as being separate from all other, but at the same time the Divine God connected each spirit as one. I was in Divine bliss.

Then it happened: my divine self started to merge. It existed, for a lack of a better word, slightly out of phase with my physical body. It wasn't the aura, for I know what that feels like. This energy body existed in the same time and space as I was in. For I saw it both in my mind's eye looking out and at the same time seeing myself from a distance looking back at me.

It was larger than my physical body. It extended itself about one foot from me all around. I felt my body falling in line. A subservient, respectful feeling came over me. I knew what it was: my divine self. This body was light. Ironically it had a consciousness with each spark, as if the light itself was alive. I felt my energy emitting from this light body and extending not only in the room I was in but for miles around us. The aura I had at that time connected with everything else. I was at one with both everything and everyone.

I felt it then—at the same time I was experiencing the wondrous beauty of this state of mind, I felt countless angels working in my midsection. Energies weaved in and out of my body. Parts of my body felt like they were being moved and adjusted. A bandage of energy began to wrap itself around my abdomen. It literally felt like an elastic wrap was tightly placed. I knew that this was intended to prevent any damage from what they did both from the external and internal energies.

It is a hard thing to explain. As I read what I wrote I feel that I cannot truly fully capture what I'm trying to relay. I feel that this event had been a healing not only of my physical self but also of my spiritual self as well. I left this place changed forever. I became a new person.

My abdomen has hurt less since then. I still get the skin pain but the degrees change from day to day. For two weeks afterwards I moved around in my life not only feeling changed and energized, but also this bandaged midsection remained with me. When I moved I felt it snuggled in place. The last thing felt when I went to bed was this wrap of light energy, and it was the first thing I felt when I woke up.

Another unexpected change was the lighter feeling within. I did not realize I had been carrying around some weight for years. I don't have a clue what it was. All I know was that it felt as if the shackles had been removed. Lighter by the experience, I became more than ever excited at the new things that are coming around the corner. Whatever they may be.

33

I Sense the Force

I intentionally excluded from the earlier chapters an event that happened in my young adult life. I felt that the meaning of it would become more apparent after I had written down some of the ideas that lay before this chapter. I wanted the foundation laid upon paper. In order to allow the proper respect that I feel it deserves, I waited till now to tell it. If you compare it to the other events in my life the magnitude of it would be minimal.

Upon further review I find this event to be the starting point of a new foundation that changed and morphed into bigger and better things. It was the beginning of my ability to feel energy waves. At the time it occurred it was a terrifying ordeal in its own right. Looking back on it and comparing it to what I experienced since then I've found it tame in comparison.

In the beginning of my quest of the Divine God I lived a monk's life. I chose a simple way of living over the finer things in life. The one exception to this rule was my rare book collection. I searched far and wide for any books on spiritual and religious pursuits, purchasing items that had gone out of print decades ago. My collection at one point filled four shelves extending sixteen feet in length. They were my pride and joy. I never had trouble finding these books. They seemed to always come into my path.

Up until this time I had no concept of what tonal vibrations were or how energy waves felt like. I did know that I was different than others. Seeing and feeling spirits was a normal thing for me. I did know that I sensed things in people I had met, but not fully understanding it I shrugged it off as nothing more than what it was. When I read a book I knew and felt that what was written had truth or not in it. Feeling the cover of a book I could quickly sense whether it contained a piece of information that I needed to find myself farther down this path I so desired.

Then it started. On one particular night I came to in some other place. I knew this was not a dream. I was standing on the first floor of a giant, rectangular room. There were bookshelves filling the outside of the walls of this building. Toward the back of the room there was a gradual ramp extending up toward the second floor. In the middle of the room there was no ceiling. I walked to the center of the first floor and looked up. I noticed that the ramp that I had originally thought headed to the second floor did not. Instead this gradual ramp wrapped around the exterior walls that continued up what would have been four floors.

I walked in a counterclockwise direction, casually strolling by books that filled the shelves. They had old leather covers with gold inlay around the bindings. Each book was a different size and shape. They had what appeared to be an inch of dust covering the surfaces. I felt like I was strolling in an antique shop looking at items with a halfhearted intent. When I reached what I would call a second floor, the books changed subtly. They were still covered in dust, but the volumes became larger. The colors on each book were more intense in nature. Reviewing each name on each book I became more interested in what they were. To this day I cannot remember the title of one book, but when I was there I remembered them in such vivid detail.

I reached the third floor. I noticed then that these books had detailed inlay patterns on each cover. Using the fingers of my right hand I gently brushed along rows of books as I walked. Not allowing my hand to be removed from them, I felt the texture and how they felt like little needle pricks on my tips of my fingers. I noticed then that the books were not the only things of interest in this building. The shelves themselves had detail carvings of patterns that wrapped all around the edge surface. I became just as amazed at the shelves as I was the books. My interested now became at full focus.

It wasn't until I reached the fourth floor that the experience became intense. Still touching the books with my right hand, I started to feel the intent behind each word that had been written in each book. Wave after wave of stabbing electricity hit the tips of my fingers, and along with it the energy of each word hit me. As I reached halfway through the fourth floor I noticed that I was being hit with not only the intent of the words that had been written in each book as I touched them but the words themselves. Some books contained similar thoughts. Both the written word and the energy behind the words were similar. Still others told totally opposite stories.

If that weren't enough, the books themselves started to pulse, as if for a split second sections of the surface of each book grew slightly, distorting its surface and moving back into position. As each wave hit, the books moved. I jerked my hand away. Looking forward I noticed I had reached the end of the ramp and at the very end were shelves of books. The waves of pulsating energy, both the words and the intent of every book I came in close proximity to, were constantly pounding my mind.

The surface of each book grew, shrank, and distorted. I realized then that these bindings of paper were alive. They had in their own right a consciousness of sorts. My mind was overloaded. I put my hands on my ears and looked up. I noticed then that the building no longer had a roof, unlike when I peered up from the first floor, seeing the ceiling as a carved wooden panel. I raised my hands in the air calling for God for help. Then I came to in my room.

I lay there for what seemed like a long time. Flashes of memories of what had happened were going through my mind. I relived this experience over and over till eventually it started to fade. I got up and started to head down the stairs toward the bathroom. As I got near the rows of books aligned along the walkway in my converted attic bedroom, I started to feel that intense energy wave.

It repeated again with another wave. Then another. As I walked closer to these books I could feel the consciousness of them. Their energy hit me. It became overwhelming. The closer I went to them the more alive they became. I saw their surfaces move and shift. Not believing what I'd just seen, I backed away. I turned around and tried to head out the door, but it started back up again. It took me four tries to pass this row of books.

These spiritual books were not the only ones that did this. Any book that I came in close contact would give me the same effect but will a lesser degree of intensity. I could tell you the intent behind the book just by touching it. I stayed away from any form of written word for weeks.

With no one to talk to, I did not know what was happening. Thinking it would disappear after a day or too, I kept my lookout and avoided books as much as I could. But those books I had never lost any intensity. So after a couple of weeks it took me a full day and many tries and trips to the dumpster to remove them from my sight. When I tossed that large volume of books out, the ability to reach what was written in each book left also.

After that occurrence I never had anything like it with that same degree of intensity. I still pick up and item and feel the energy signature that had been left on it. I can tell you if it came from the person using it. I can feel the person who created it or the intent behind the words. I don't like used items. It bothers me. Old items have too much energy embedded in them for me to handle. I find I have to wash my hands to remove most of the energy that leaches off of an item onto my hands.

When I purchased a new truck from a local dealer, I spent three months feeling the energies of the person who assembled the steering wheel into the vehicle. I dealt with this problem by wearing gloves till eventually the energies of this man disappeared. If I did not use protection, whenever I touched the steering wheel I saw him, the condition of his health and his mindset. All, which I hate to say, wasn't in a healthy state. I avoid touching items in stores for that same reason.

I cannot grab just anything and get something from it. It usually comes when I least expect it. The energies are usually in an excited state, either good or bad. One time I purchased a used game machine then promptly gave it away to someone else because I could not take the energies of the person who had used it prior to me.

I feel that this jump-started my ability to feel energy waves and patterns. They are similar in nature, but my ability changed and evolved to what I use now. The remnant of it still exists today, though thankfully not to the degree I experienced many years in the past.

34

Are You Looking At Me?

It took me many years to formulate an image that I could relay to you on how these energy waves feel to me. Take a drop of water and allow it to hit a surface of a body of water. You see the wave ripple outward. Now let's see multiple drops of water hitting the surface. The ripples push outward in all directions. It is only when it comes in contact with another ripple heading toward it that the waves on both drops change. The change in direction and motion of each wave is dependent upon the opposing force and mass of the incoming wave. When you multiply this by a large number of drops of water hitting the surface a fraction of a second apart, the surface of the water changes and becomes very interesting to watch.

Look into a crowd of people. Try to visualize a wave of sorts emitting out from each individual. This wave heads out in all directions. It is only when it comes in contact with another living energy signature that it mixes with it and changes direction. The strength of the other incoming wave determines how much each pulsating wave mixes and changes. These waves can be from humans, animals, plants, Mother Nature, and to a lesser degree inanimate objects as well. We are all affected by these waves intertwining with our own.

A pulsating wave for me has a multi-part effect on my mind. I feel the energies moving out from each person in the room. I feel how they move and intertwine with other moving waves. I feel the strength as each wave pulses. As each wave is being emitted, I feel the strength behind it. Finally I feel, on occasion, a slight trace of sound within each wave. The combination of all this adds a mental image that I'm inside a fast, turbulent river. I feel areas where the current is moving smoother, where it's faster, and where there are many rocks causing a thickening of the energies. I can at times feel the air change around me as if I was moving through hardening mud.

One gift, a by-product of years in feeling the Divine God, has allowed me a unique ability. I can sense most of the time when someone is looking at me. If I am conscious of them looking I sense it and do not turn around. Most of the times, without realizing it, I start to zone out. The only thing I'm aware of is the feeling of the change in the waves of energy around me. My mind finds a fast-flowing area and follows it. I can usually turn to a person when they've just glanced toward my direction. Often times I will look toward the person seconds prior to them turning their head and looking my way. In these times I'm not aware that I am staring at them. When I come to, I realize I have been staring at them. I never know how long I've gazed at them. They become uncomfortable and usually turn away quickly.

About one third of the time our minds link on some level. At that time I sense their mood, their energy shifts, and sometimes on occasion I have been able to sense what they are thinking of. People have told me that when this happens they start to feel like they're zoning out. Some of them also have asked me if I read their mind. Of course I reassure them I cannot. It is an interesting feeling when this happens. I never get tired of it.

Because of this and the sensing of energy waves, I do not like crowds. I have avoided concerts and large gatherings because of the intensity I feel. Of course I cannot tell anyone of this. Few people would truly understand, and fewer yet would actually know what it feels like. I have never found any other who has the same type of ability. I can only hope that this gift increases over time.

35

It's Been Not Only an Exalted But a Lonely Life as Well

As with anything in life, the degree to which a person experiences success is dependent upon how much energy they put into it. The more energy one directs toward a goal the less the energy is spent in other areas. Generally if it is a career you want, steps are taken to achieve it. If it is a family you might spend your energies in that direction. Others will learn to divide their energies evenly among their personal life, career, friends, and hobbies. There really is no wrong way to divide your energy. If your cosmic self desires experiences in one area of life, you will naturally gravitate toward it.

I had no choice in the area I would be spending my life with. I came into the physical reality knowing that a lifetime of a career, family, friends, and financial security wasn't for me. Don't get me wrong—I would not mind if I had any one of them. At times I do desire a family, good friends, and a well-paying job. I knew that in order to achieve what my mind had in mind regarding my spiritual progression toward the Divine

God, I had to forsake certain luxuries that most people have chosen. Traveling a spiritual journey takes large amounts of energy. It is not uncommon to spend months in meditation, contemplation, and reflection in order to receive a small portion of enlightenment. It would take me months to raise my vibrations to a point and only have it removed within a few moments of laying of hands on a person. It is not a path that many would choose.

I have always felt more comfortable with the other side. There is not a moment in my day that I don't desire the return home. I feel that this life is my exile. When I have lived in the other realms as much as my higher self would allow, my energies change. People look at me differently. Relationships have always been my downfall. Whether it is Divinely sent or my higher self setting up blocks to allow as much energy toward my spiritual goals I cannot say. All I can do is look at my life and notice patterns within it. I watched my relationships fall apart time and time again, many times through no fault of my own. I don't think I could have done the things I have, if I had not shut down these areas to concentrate on what was needed.

Things never came easy for me. I have always had to work for it. Once I found that flowing current I would try to ride it for as long as I could. It truly is a lonely life. I have seen many wondrous things. I have many angels and guides around me. I feel them. I see them. I talk to them. I could not imagine my life without them. It is like they are on one side of the glass and I am on the other. Yes, we see each other but the physical contact still remains illusive. Feeling the tonal vibrations and energies brings me to states of euphoria. It is at times like a drug addiction, waiting for the next time I'll receive the long waited fix. In the end I experience these things by myself.

We are humans. Because of this we need various degrees of social contact. By the sheer nature of our biological beings the desire to express our emotions and to open ourselves to another is something we need to survive. In some ways a spiritual journey is opposite from this. It is a path of self-discovery. You spend many days, weeks, and months pursuing this path alone. It does take a toll on your physical mindset. You find yourself wanting to go farther and higher than you went last time. Yet, you know that in order to obtain this, the energy needed must be taken from somewhere. You convince yourself that you have plenty of time to redirect the required energies back into other areas once you have obtained your desires. That really never happens. As you find bigger and better pieces, you still yearn for more.

I don't regret my decision about my path. It is something I decided I would do before coming into this physical reality. I just don't think I realized the extent of the sacrifices I would be making. As I age with each passing moment, time has come and gone, and I have missed out on a lot of things. Would I do it again? Yes. Is there anything I would have changed? No. The outcome would have been the same. Please don't misunderstand me—the things I have seen, words have a hard time describing. I just wish I could share these experiences in ways other than writing them upon paper. For words only describe a small portion of the whole experience.

Your thought patterns change. Interacting with others becomes harder in areas that are not spiritual in nature. Your roles with friends who come into your life are different. They arrive when they need something in their life and leave when it is completed. You become a nomad of sorts, wandering in this physical realm and interacting with people on few occasions. You have a hard time sharing things that excite and stimulate your mind. People generally want to interact with you about physical things that happen in their lives, about common events. They would think you strange if you started sharing events that are in other realms. If you shared enough of these they may even have you admitted into a mental institution.

I have not figured out up to this point in my life how to balance these areas in my life. Whenever I try to do so I find my situation screwing up. I have tried denying my spiritual journey, and that had caused me suffering and pain. I have also denied my physical self, and to a lesser degree I still suffered. There is no easy answer—none that I could find, anyway.

But it is a journey worth taking. The height of enlightenment far outweighs the sorrow. What I do find is those ideas and concept that mold and become the foundation of your belief system are so far from mainstream thinking that you become an island of truth. You want someone to land there and, even if only for a moment in time, understand what you have learned. You hope they will take what feels right for them and head upon their own journey.

36

She Arrives, and then She Leaves

I had a hard time deciding whether to put this chapter in this book and allow my inner self only to be exposed once more or to leave what I'm about to write out. It cut me deeply. Like everything else, I will heal from it, but the scars will remain with me for a long time. It is in some ways painful for me to write it down.

I can only hope it will be an ointment to heal these wounds, therapy given to relieve the sorrow I feel about what had happened. It represents my feeble attempts to understand why it happened and what was the true purpose for the events that led up to it.

As far back as I can remember, I have always known of a soul that would come into my life. Seeing her in vision after vision burned these details into my mind's eye, and they've remained with me throughout my life. I knew what color her hair was, how the shape of it flowed around her head and down upon her shoulders. Her physical appearance, the shape of her lips, arms, torso, and legs, I knew all too well. What she did for a living. How many kids she had.

When she was married and then divorced. I knew that we had lived together in many lifetimes prior to this one. I remember her energies from the other side before we ventured upon this physical realm. All this stayed with me through the years. On occasion she would come into my dreams. We would talk but upon awakening I never remembered what she said.

As I grew older she also grew, aging along with me. I first thought it was an angel who had been with me in my life. As I grew older I began to understand the subtle shift of energy and realized that it was a spirit upon this earth. Feelings of her were so strong at times I thought she was just around the corner and that we would meet. Of course that never happened in my earlier days.

I knew that if we would just sit down and compare our lives we would notice that the both of us were never far apart. Having shared similar events along the way was both a blessing and a curse at times. Feeling her so real in my mind and yet not being able to touch, hold, and talk to her, my heart felt pain at times.

I became discouraged in the last few years. She had never left. I had medium friends bring up her energy from time to time. They reconfirmed what I knew all along. In the first half of my life I used the knowledge that she was arriving in my life at some point. I would tell myself not to spend much time in dating because I did not want to betray our love. I did date throughout my life.

I have had beautiful souls and good relationships, but for the most part my heart waited for the right one to come along. I knew she was there. I could tell that she needed to grow in one area or another, what she needed to experience. I felt that both our energies would have to change to allow that connection I so desired.

Throughout my life not only have I seen her current state, I've also seen pieces of our future life together. I saw the child who would come within the first year of dating. I saw the marriage, my life all wrapped up in a nice little package. I put off my yearning for someone, knowing that I would receive this at some time or another. I concentrated my energies on my spiritual journey, buying time till the joyous event would arrive.

I believe that, because of the uncertainty in life, we agree prior to coming here that each of us will have a couple potential relationships. I don't think we would hinge all our hopes and dreams on one person. I know for myself I had agreed with at least three souls on the other side for potential relationships upon this physical realm.

I can feel them out there, but not to the degree I felt the connection with this one. As time went along and years passed, my love for her grew. It was not an imaginary person my mind made up to compensate for the lack of energy I put into this area. She was as real to me as anyone around me.

I explained in chapter thirteen a vision I had with a woman and my life with her; this was that person. Details flooding in at that time only confirmed things I saw throughout my life. She was everything to me. I knew she would arrive, eventually. So I waited patiently for her arrival.

I still kept my eyes open for other potential relationships, but when they would arrive I knew right there that not only weren't they this woman in my dreams, their energies were not compatible with mine. I was not comparing them to her. This was not the case.

Then the day arrived. I was at a gathering I regularly attended. Lost in my own thoughts, I started to feel this energy wave change around me. A familiar feeling came over me. I followed it through my mind's eye and traced it to a vehicle driving down the road toward the building.

I knew this sensation, but I had never approached it before in this lifetime. Then they walked in. I knew she did not recognize me, but a connection was made. A thread that had been attached from my higher self to hers ignited with energy. At this time I could only see the back of her. Desperately wanting to look at her but not wanting to be compulsive about it, I waited patiently till the proceedings ended. I bided my time after this function to find my way toward her.

I went into the room and looked over toward her beautiful face. As attractive as she was, this paled in comparison to what I saw within. My mind split into two. The physical conscious state went into automatic pilot as my mind expanded to this new level of awareness. Deeper and deeper I went. I saw her Divine self.

The light was a refined, brilliant white. Mixed in with it was pulsating wave after wave of her tonal sound, which was far too familiar to me. I saw the effect of my energies mixing with hers. Her higher Divine light flared up with intensity and brilliance upon feeling my energies. Recognition on some level hit her.

I zoned out. Still faintly aware of my surrounding but in full conscious mode of this heightened state, I relived lifetimes past spent with her, what she was on the other side, and our future together.

In those few short seconds I had lived lifetime and lifetime with her. I'd experienced the love we shared and the understanding we felt between us. When I finally returned it had felt like I had been gone for hundreds of years. I felt like a man who had lost his partner of many years only to find her years later still alive but with no memory of him.

As the next couple of months passed her connection was strong with me. Many times a day I would get her energies reaching out to me. I sensed her mind-state and thoughts. Lovingly I would send my energies back. When we got together I had a hard time staying in the physical realm.

I kept having my conscious self go more into the energetic realm. I kept feeling how our energies intertwined together, and I knew that on some level she recognized it. I saw that because of this, her abilities would start to open in the spirit realm. From the moment I saw her I felt we were married.

I did not care what life she had lived up to this point. It did not matter what problems she and her children were going through. I have never felt so alive with another as I did with her. I told myself I would take it slow. I did not want to mess this opportunity up.

The moment I saw her mother and sister I recognized many lifetimes with them. I knew how they interacted with her, what roles each had played in each lifetime, and how my interaction was with them at that time. I saw one lifetime where she was the wife of my brother. My brother and I were sailors. He was the deliver of goods, and I was the traveling healer. It was tough to feel so close but not be able to express the joy and love I had for her in this lifetime toward her.

On some level she recognized this connection also. She would occasionally express the concern that I was reading her mind. You don't live these moments in time with someone and not be of the same type of energy. I knew, based upon her energies, what her mind-state was. Her worries and problems would flash before me. At the same time I would see our life together. If it were up to me, I would have been more than happy to marry her right on the spot. I loved her, and to some degree still do. I wanted to tell her everything.

What I saw and felt. What was in our future if she wanted it. How our life would turn out. I yearned so much to express these emotions and the desire I had toward her. Of course I held all that in. I knew that she would have a hard enough time dealing with these energies that had ignited between us. Her kids felt like my kids. I got along with them very well. I enjoyed her mother and sister's company.

The first two times I saw her daughter she had brownish skin. When I looked at her daughter I would see long, straight, jet-black hair and a round face. The memories of Persia would flash in my mind's eye. It wasn't till the third time when she came over with her daughter that I realized that she did not look remotely like that.

There was no long, black hair. Her skin was not brown, and her face was not oval. I usually get flashes of faces that distort a person's own image. These would only last for a second and then disappear. Her appearance was different. It remained with her the first two times I saw her. It wasn't till the third time, when I saw her in a different location, that I noticed what she looked like in this life.

I began to sense an energy shift a couple of weeks prior to Christmas. It takes me a while to figure out where the energy changes will manifest. Sometimes it's within my own life. Other times it's with friends and family, and still other times it is on a global scale. Wherever it was coming from, I did not like it. About a week prior to Christmas I had a chance to see her. At this time her energies were completely different.

She felt withdrawn and pulled back. A repulsive feeling, I felt. As I tried to reach out with my energetic self I could feel her energies jerk back. It was as if a light switch had just clicked. She tried to avoid me, not wanting to talk. This was not like her. Chalking it up to something happening in her life, I backed off. This did not end here. The plans we had for this holiday season came crashing down. When we would find ourselves meeting by chance in public, she would have a terrified look on her face. Avoiding me, she would gain as much distance from me as possible.

I did not understand this. Only a few weeks' prior things were going great. I kept my peace on what I was experiencing. I made sure what I said and did was the best way possible I could to keep this relationship going.

It took me a few days to put all the pieces together. Instead of coming out and telling me that she no longer wanted to see me, she took another route instead. There were only a couple of times in my life I hit bottom. I spent my days after that crying in bed. The pain and loss I felt was immeasurable. My body shook. I did not want to eat. I relived the loss in many lifetimes and on many levels.

I had no one I could talk to. I felt completely alone—abandoned again by everything and everyone. The pain got so intense my chest hurt. My joints ached, and my muscles were sore. I could not believe that, after all these years of seeing her, this had happened. It made no sense. No matter how many times I rearranged the pieces, they would not form anything that I could understand. I became alarmed, and in only a few short days my body started to break down. I felt like I was dying.

I knew then I had to do something or I would not be here long. I needed to harden my being if only for a short while. I needed to toughen up and allow this not to affect me. If I could look at it as being only in this lifetime, then things had not gotten to a point to warrant my reaction. If you factor in what I experienced and re-lived, then that idea had some merit.

It is hard dealing with some events that happen in your life. It is even harder when you see this person on occasion. We share the same interests. The pain is still felt when her energies come in contact with mine. I have to deal with it every time we see each other. I am happy that it did not affect her like it did me.

I have seen that she has moved on with her life in ignorance of how she had affected my life. This is good. A piece of me is still a little bit burned by the experience. I only wish I could have bounced back with such resilience as she had done. I asked my angels and guides why, but no answer has come. The only rational explanation I can come to terms with is I needed to let go of this piece of me to move on into something more beneficial to me. I don't know if this is right, but it is the answer that allows me some comfort.

I have noticed that my meditation and healing skills have been greatly reduced while I deal with the healing of this event in my life. It seems that the more you delve into the energies of others the more they in turn have an effect on your own.

37

Living Many Lives at the Same Time

This started like my usual trips to the other side. I started in an old-style farmhouse. Looking around I noticed that this house had been heavily used at one point. There were broken pieces of furniture and junk lying around. Judging by the amount of dust and cobwebs around the place I figured it had not been lived in for a long while. I asked my angels who owned this place. They replied that the landlord that owned this area did. They also told me that it was my time to stay here in the house.

I set off to clean this mess up. I made it the most comfortable living space I could under the circumstances. As I started to work my way toward the back of the house I noticed an old, locked door. I asked my angels where this door led. They replied, "To the truth."

With some effort and a little prying I finally popped the lock off the door and opened it. I looked in. It appeared to be a small, oddly shaped closet. My angels told me to go in. So I did. In the middle of this room hung a pull chain attached to a dimly lit bulb. I clicked on the light. The door slammed shut behind me.

Looking around for a way to reopen the door I noticed an old, rusted button sticking out from the wall on one side of this closet. I pushed it. Instead of opening the door, the room started to creak and shake. I became startled. My angels reassured me it was ok. The room slowly started to lower into the ground, leaving the walls in place. What replaced the walls was carved rock formations. This elevator groaned and creaked along for what seem like minutes.

When the elevator finally stopped and the floor settled into its new location, the door on the other side came into view. I opened it. Walking through it I felt I had walked back in time. The structure I came into had an Amish look and feel to it. Its beams were tightly locked in place with each other.

Attaching beams together were thick, round, wooden dowels. The building was amazing. I felt I had stepped back into the 1700s. It appeared to be a factory. Cubicles were spread along each row. People worked diligently in each cubicle. There were all different types and shapes of people. They were tall, thin, young, old, male, female, and many different types of races. They were all busily working on their assigned tasks. They worked in conjunction with each other as if they were a finely tuned and well oiled machine.

My angels told me to look around. So I did. I was amazed at the efficiency at each person working. Not one person was doing the same as another. They would occasionally walk from their cubicle to another's then back again. For the most part they stayed in their assigned work area. I realized then that the outfits they wore came from different time periods. None looked from the same time. I knew then that my angels wanted me to come to a revelation of some kind and I need to place the pieces together.

I asked my guides if I could talk to them. They replied, yes. So I approached a middle-aged woman and asked what she was doing. She replied that the landlord needed this task done and that she'd volunteered for it. As I talked to her and others I began to realize that each one of them felt familiar to me. They looked different and spoke differently but they had the same quality about them. I did know from their replies they were all trying to get things ready for the landlord's arrival.

I walked to the end of the building, slid the big bay doors open, and looked out. There was an old-time village in the back of this factory. I noticed the blue sky with the small packets of clouds. I also felt the urgency of this landlord's arrival. I asked my angels if the elevator still attached to this building and did it still head back to the farmhouse. They replied that it did. I stood there pondering what I saw and heard.

I did know that there was something that was deeply pressing upon me. I knew that my angels would answer my questions, but I had to pose it to them first. It had to come from within. The revelation needed to be brought forth first. So I stood there looking at this village, running the events that had just happened through my mind, while my angels calmly waited behind me.

It hit me all of a sudden. I understood what this place was. I knew why it had been shown to me this way and why I had to go through it like I did. I turned around wide-eyed and called for my angels. I asked them whether those people in that building were the lives I have lived in different times in history. They replied yes. I said that I lived multiple lifetimes and that what I remembered throughout my life was true. My angels smiled. Then I said that the landlord was my cosmic self.

The accumulation of all I was, had been, and will be. They replied, "You're correct." My angels then replied that because I live in a linear plane these lives would be considered past, present, and future. But when you look at it with your cosmic self you reach beyond space and time. You begin to see it as running many lifetimes simultaneously.

They told me that the house represented my current life I'm living. I am a foreman of sorts in it. Even though I feel isolated underneath I'm connected to all the experiences and knowledge of what every lifetime brought. Each person underneath in that factory had his or her moment in the farmhouse.

In this moment of time it is my turn in it. The village represented to me my life on the other side. The accumulation of it all was my cosmic self. We split into many different aspects of ourselves to learn things that our cosmic self desires to learn to fulfill its full potential. The urgency I experienced was that all the lifetimes I have lived and am living are coming to an end. There will not be many more, if any, my cosmic self will need to learn in this physical realm. This I was thankful for.

38

Multiple Lifetimes — You Can't Be Serious

Originally, in writing about multiple lifetimes I was going to leave this chapter out. A couple of months had passed and I could not get the images and ideas that hung around in my conscious and subconscious mind to leave. Their stubbornness became a spike that had been repeatedly pounded into the front of my thoughts until I came to the realization that I had to attempt to express what I feel on paper. Trying to explain these theories that I take as truth in my life will not be an easy one. Laying them on paper no matter how hard I try will only be a tainted and a partial image at best. So please bear with me on this. I will do my best to express as closely as I can how I see them.

When we live in this physical reality we call life, we are governed by its rules and laws of physics. Pieces of ourselves have been split into many smaller parts and reside close to each other through the many planes and realities back toward our Divine and cosmic self. The smallest piece of it is located in the physical realm. We are stripped of the conscious knowledge of our own God self. Our abilities and realizations that we create our physical surroundings and understanding in the process are consciously removed. We are constantly feeling apart or separated from something or someone. We fill this emptiness as best as we can by experiencing what brings us joy and happiness.

If this were the only effect we had in dealing with this physical plane that would be enough. Because we are on a journey of finding our own Divine self, we needed to set up governing rules to allow this process to be a series of self-discoveries. The limitation of our mind needed a set of tangible rules to guide us. We perceive time as linear. A past, present, and future with a series of steps needed to be built upon themselves so our consciousness could grow and develop into what it seeks. We look upon life as a finite series of events. It has a beginning, middle, and finally an end. Experiences in life have repeatedly pounded these reconfirming ideas of this pathway upon which we walk during this journey.

The abstract idea I have proposed in the previous chapters regarding a linear timeframe not existing outside of this physical reality is itself is a hard pill to swallow. When you expand your awareness just remotely that there is something more than what we perceive as real, then this idea may not seem so remote as it once had. Let's imagine for a moment that time is not linear.

There is no past or future, just the present. Look at this exact moment right now, as you're reading these words on paper. If the past is but a perception of events and the future is but the accumulation of what we experience, then the moment is the expression of who we are. If we view ourselves not walking on this path of life but instead standing motionless and the path is encompassing everything all around us, we begin to see life differently. Viewing it with a new set of awareness allows us to gain a little piece of our Divine and cosmic self and mold it into the physical conscious being.

Let's take this idea a little further. You know you can change your future by what you do and perceive in the present. No one will argue with you on that. You also know that who you are is based not so much on the events that have transpired but the perception of your awareness when they did. That is who you are in the now. If you allow yourself to become aware that this is not a linear procession but instead a series of events that are currently being lived in the moment, you can in turn change the past and also change the future. We're not talking about removing an event that has transpired but instead change the perception of that event in our consciousness. We can allow that two-way communication between both past and future. We can in turn affect the only reality we live in, the present. By changing the observation or reaction of a traumatic event in the past we in turn change who we are in the present. We are in essence affecting and changing the series of linear events.

Stripping off the old perceptions of what we know as truth from generations and generations is a hard one. When you start to learn how these higher truths operate into the physical realm you begin to take back pieces of your own Divine self. You take ownership of them and in turn become a creator in the reality that surrounds you. Working with new energies and understanding how they operate and interact in this plane, you become co-creators with the Divine God. It's the next step in evolution.

As I have expressed before, the cosmic self is the accumulation of all past, present, and future in not only this lifetime but also in every lifetime you have lived. Both on this physical plane and in all the others, taking the concept of living these lives simultaneously, you realize that everything is interlinked with each other. You start to realize that not only can you affect the outcome of the current physical reality, you also can affect the others lives you're experiencing at this moment in the now. You can also draw upon the energies of those consciousnesses and use them to mold changes on multi-dimensional level, that will in turn have a direct effect in your surroundings.

Drawing up upon experiences in other lifetimes and realities, you can obtain greater reservoirs of energy to mold this existing reality into a more tangible, joyful, and enriched life. Because you are linked with every aspect of yourself in every reality, what you change will change those lives as well. Moving back and forth through this link you're able to expand your mind and awareness to deeper and higher truths. The prospects are limitless. Expanding your mind even farther allows you do reach into the past and draw upon the DNA of your cellular structure prior to an illness and re-program the disease cells back into the state it had been prior to the event itself. You can lessen pain and even eliminate it if enough thought and energy is drawn from the threads that join all the present existences we are experiencing now. You can even stop the linear thinking of aging and allow the cells to maintain a youthful state.

The limitations in how far we can take this is largely due to the restrictions our mind has set upon itself. Freed from this predetermined, linear way of thinking we can become the Divine self we were intended to be. We can change the path under our feet with each change in thought itself. You cannot change another person's reality. But the reality that surrounds you can be changed and molded with each minor jump from a linear way of thinking to way of ideas and perceptions that exists outside of it.

By removing the thinking that the path of life is linear and bringing to the forefront of your consciousness the idea that you're not a point on this path that has a beginning and end, you start to see how energies itself interact and work with each other. You start to realize that you're standing motionless on top of this path. Waves of thought energy emit in a three-hundred-and-sixty-degree circle around yourself.

As each thought changes, the path you have around yourself begins to mold into something different. The ground is constantly liquefying and then hardening into something different under your feet. This happening every time a thought you use is the non-linear way of thinking. So your surroundings and physical reality is changed. Time becomes non-existent. If you don't like the wave that's being emitted, then by reaching out and tapping into these hidden reservoirs of energy you can change your reality by resending the necessary code to re-program your truth. You need to realize that when you obtain the state of non-linear thought it only has to be sent out once. If done correctly the effects can reach its necessary target in the past, future, and the present.

Another idea I like to have applied to this new way of thinking is the ability to send Divine energy to different spots along this linear time frame. You can also send this energy to other lives as well. By understanding these rules that govern the linear pathway you can then understand how to circumvent them. You can direct Divine energy beyond these limitations and allow it to boomerang back into this pathway in areas where you will need the most support.

This means sending these energy waves both to past or future events. Doing this alone can change the destiny that your mind had laid out prior to these events. You're taking ownership in your own life and not allowing predestiny to have any influence on any part of this path you have chosen.

39

The Last Chapter

I did not think that this book would be so hard to end. What I realized in writing this manuscript is that it became my confessor of sorts. It allowed me to express ideas, emotions, and theories that I had kept to myself for all my life. When I started writing fragments of my life, I never thought I would have had so much information to share. I worried at first that if I could fill fifty pages it would have been a miracle. Fortunately that was not the case. As each story was put into a coherent set of words I found that three more I had forgotten about took its place. I wanted to spill my soul as completely as I could in hopes that I could find links that would not only give me a greater understanding about myself but the knowledge I had with the Divine goals.

If I told you I wanted to write this to help others that may run across similar experiences, to let them know they are not crazy, to tell them that they need to confront these things and understand them for what they are, I would be truthful in saying that. But that was not the only case. I did have an ulterior motive. I did not fully understand it at that time. I needed to grab parts of my life and bring them forward.

I needed to splice these pieces together and create a moving projection of events that I could review. Totally separate events that did not seem related came together and formed a new, completed picture. New revelations were revealed. Deeper insights were created. Things came together, and a new level of awareness formed. I understood why things had happen in my life, and I was fortunate to realize this in my consciousness prior to passing from this physical reality.

I did not realize that I was very fortunate in what was given to me. At times it felt like a burden. Even though I don't fully understand every piece of it, I am glad that things have fallen the way they have. I have enjoyed not only the ability to work in the physical realm but also the opportunity to scratch the surface of many others.

Nothing is perfect. In our impressions of and reactions to situations that arrive, we as humans never see the clear truth in anything. That is ok. I have found what feels like a sure-footed ground in my life. My truth resonates from me with understanding and knowledge that has allowed me to find my place in all things. Isn't that the real reason for living? To understand who and what we are and how to reach what we need to become? At least for me it is the case.

I have never regained most of my memory. That is ok as well. I have learned to accept it for what it is and move on. I still have the pain, but through medication and the new way of drawing cellular structures through, I have been able to minimize the feeling to a more managed way of life.

I can appreciate things more. I deal with what comes my way on a daily bases and try to not let things bother me to the degree they once did. I'm still learning and hope that part of my life never ends. Finding new routes to many different destinations both in this physical reality and the other planes fills me with newfound joy. Molding energies on a sub-atomic level and pulling them through into this reality becomes meaningful in my life. I can only hope that a piece in this book helps you in your search for your Divine self and how you fit in the grandeur scheme of God's Divine plan. I truly from the deepest parts of my heart thank you for attempting to understand what I find is truth.

Printed in the United Kingdom
by Lightning Source UK Ltd.
135778UK00002B/125/P